GreenSpirit book series

Awakening to
EARTH-CENTRED
CONSCIOUSNESS
SELECTION FROM GREENSPIRIT MAGAZINE

Edited by Ian Mowll
and Santoshan (Stephen Wollaston)

With contributions by
Richard Adams, Jean Boulton, Susan Canney, Chris Clarke,
Erna Colebrook, Victoria Field, Jean Francis, Jonathan Furst,
Katie Hill, Amelia Kinkade, Margaret Lee, Nigel Lees,
Marian Van Eyk McCain, Nicola Peel, June Raymond
and Piers Warren

CreateSpace Independent Publishing Platform
Distributed by CreateSpace

Title No. 9 in the GreenSpirit Book Series
www.greenspirit.org.uk

ISBN 9798785727496 (hardback) / 9781986435017 (paperback)
© Ian Mowll and Santoshan (Stephen Wollaston) 2018
GreenSpirit eBook Series edition also available

All rights reserved. Except for brief quotations in critical articles or reviews, no part of this book may be reproduced in any manner without prior written permission from the authors.

Design and artwork by Santoshan (Stephen Wollaston)
Printed by CreateSpace and Amazon

Picture Credits:
Front cover image © Violetkaipa/Shutterstock.com
Page 26 painting by June Witheridge, reproduced with permission of the owner of the painting
Page 37 and 38 photo © Vanessa Clark
Page 79 and 80 © Keith Dodson/Shutterstock.com
Page 86 © Katie Hill
Page 121 © Nicola Peel
Page 125 and 126 © Serif Image Collection 5
Page 147 and 148 © Vanessa Clark

Contents

Editors' Preface 7

Introduction, *Santoshan (aka Stephen Wollaston)* 9

PART ONE: INTERACTIONS WITH NATURE

1. The Old Woman and the Sea, *Erna Colebrook* 15

2. The Black Mamba, *Amelia Kinkade* 21

3. Earth Activist Training, Permaculture, and Simple Techniques for Saving the World! *Jonathan Furst* 29

PART TWO: BALANCE AND HEALING

4. Living on the Edge: A View Through the Lens of Complexity, *Jean Boulton* 39

5. Healing Our Cities, *Marian Van Eyk McCain* 47

6. The Healing Garden: A Personal Tribute to the Work of Pioneering Transpersonal Therapist Jenny Grut (1955 – 2006), *Richard Adams* 55

7. Wild Thing, You Make My Heart Sing: Animal Poetry and Ecopsychology, *Victoria Field* 65

8. The Paws that Heal, *Margaret Lee* 73

PART THREE: IMPLEMENTING GREEN WISDOM

9. Project Green Hands, *Katie Hill* 81

10. Elephant Protection: An Interview with Susan Canney, *Ian Mowll* 89

11. Spirituality and Veganism, *Piers Warren* 99

12. Down to Earth: An Eco-Friendly Burial, *Jean Francis* 107

13. Eco-Restaurant in the Amazon Jungle: An Interview with Nicola Peel, *Ian Mowll* 117

PART FOUR: NATURE'S POWERS AND WONDERS

14. Living in the Paradox of Destruction and Creation, *Chris Clarke* 127

15. The Oak Child, *Nigel Lees* 135

16. The Hurricane, *June Raymond* 143

GREENSPIRIT RESOURCES

GreenSpirit Book Series and Other Resources 147

Editors' Preface

This is the ninth title in the GreenSpirit Book Series, which is a low-cost series sold at production price only. *Awakening to Earth-Centred Consciousness* brings together a collection of insightful articles and two inspiring interviews from GreenSpirit magazine. For details about current titles in the series, please see the Resources section at the back of this book.

GreenSpirit is a registered charity based in the UK. The main contents/written material, editing, design and promotional work for our books is done on a purely voluntary basis or given freely by contributors who share our passion for Gaia-centred spirituality.

* * *

Editors' Note

For the purpose of clarity, quotations used in passages by the author of a chapter are placed in double quotation marks. Words given stress by the author of a chapter, which are not quotations, are either in single quotation marks or italic.

Introduction

I do not think the measure of a civilization is how tall its buildings of concrete are, but rather how well its people have learned to relate to their environment and fellow human beings.
– Sun Bear of the Chippewa Tribe[1]

The natural world is the larger sacred community to which we belong.
– Thomas Berry[2]

It amazes me how much the idea of globalisation is talked about these days and how the notion of plundering Earth's natural resources and making, selling and buying more stuff is still held up as an ultimate for progress, economic stability and growth. Not only is it short-sighted, as the Earth is obviously not some kind of magical store cupboard that will miraculously keep filling itself up, but it overlooks the rights of the more-than-human queendoms and kingdoms, as well as the rights of indigenous people inhabiting regions of the world where profits can be made by a privileged few. There is a clear breakdown in acknowledging how all species and people are our brothers and sisters. And just as we would naturally care about and for our closest blood family members, there is an essential spiritual need to care about our wider global family.

Like other GeenSpirit publications, this book highlights this important message and reminds us about acknowledging and embracing our more-than-human relations. GreenSpirit magazine, from which all the chapters of this book have been compiled, has from its humble beginnings continually aimed to raise awareness of the interrelatedness we have with all people and life. The magazine started out three decades ago under the name 'Interchange', which had a simple format of news items, poems and articles with line drawings for images, produced by the Centre for Creation Spirituality at St James's Church, Piccadilly.[3] It then became known by its current title in 1999 and gradually took on the appearance of a more traditional magazine.

The articles and interviews selected for this book share personal stories, engage thoughtfully with green topics, and provide insightful teachings about the interconnectedness we have with the natural world. The book is divided into four parts: (1) Interactions with Nature, (2) Balance and Healing, (3) Implementing Green Wisdom, and (4) Nature's Powers and Wonders. The stories and teachings in the chapters frequently seek to motivate us to interact skilfully with life, live compassionately and face the challenges of Earth-centred living with deep awareness.

The articles and interviews, which Ian Mowll and I have selected, span a recent period of 11 years. The chapters themselves are not planned to be read linearly from front to back. You as the reader may wish to start at any place that draws your attention. I personally feel there are insights here for everyone – for the more academically minded to newcomers to the fields of eco-spirituality and green wisdom – covering a wide range of major subjects such as green burials, veganism, raising green awareness in the Amazon, elephant protection, ecopsychology, personal encounters with animal friends, and how Nature can heal us.

For me, the contents of this book represent some of the most thoughtful pieces that have appeared in GreenSpirit magazine though I'm sure other members of GreenSpirit and readers of the magazine will think of alternatives that could also have been included. The insights within the following pages often encourage us to embrace an inclusive and caring spirituality – one that encompasses living the whole of our lives as wisely as we can and manifests qualities that lead us to recognising profound levels of life and Nature, of which we are all wondrously interwoven and a part, and the essential obligations this brings for responsible Gaia-centred living.

These days green educationists, Earth-centred spiritual seekers and eco-activists are only too aware that we humans currently stand at a crucial position of deciding whether to become jointly involved or not in respecting the rights of all species, preserving Nature's essential balance and the making of a new Earth community. A compassion for Earth and all her species is called for – to recognise all as a sacred whole with profound meaning and purpose. As it is through awakening to Nature's sacredness and importance that we begin to care for the diversity of life that Mother Earth has sought to celebrate.

Overall, the fourteen articles and two interviews in this book left me with a sense of hope for what we can awaken to and collectively achieve and embody in our lives. I can only trust that others will find the following pages equally encouraging and beneficial in their quests for an Earth-centred consciousness and the enrichment of life it can potentially bring for all.

– Santoshan (aka Stephen Wollaston)

References
1. Sun Bear of the Chippewa Tribe. In Wayne Teasdale's *The Mystic Hour: A Day Book of Interspiritual Wisdom and Devotion*, New World Library, 2004.
2. Berry, Thomas. *Dream of the Earth*, Sierra Club Books, 1990.
3. Griffiths, Petra. *The Creation Spirituality Movement in the UK: The Early Years*, GreenSpirit magazine, Winter 2006, 8:3.

* * *

PART ONE
INTERACTIONS WITH NATURE

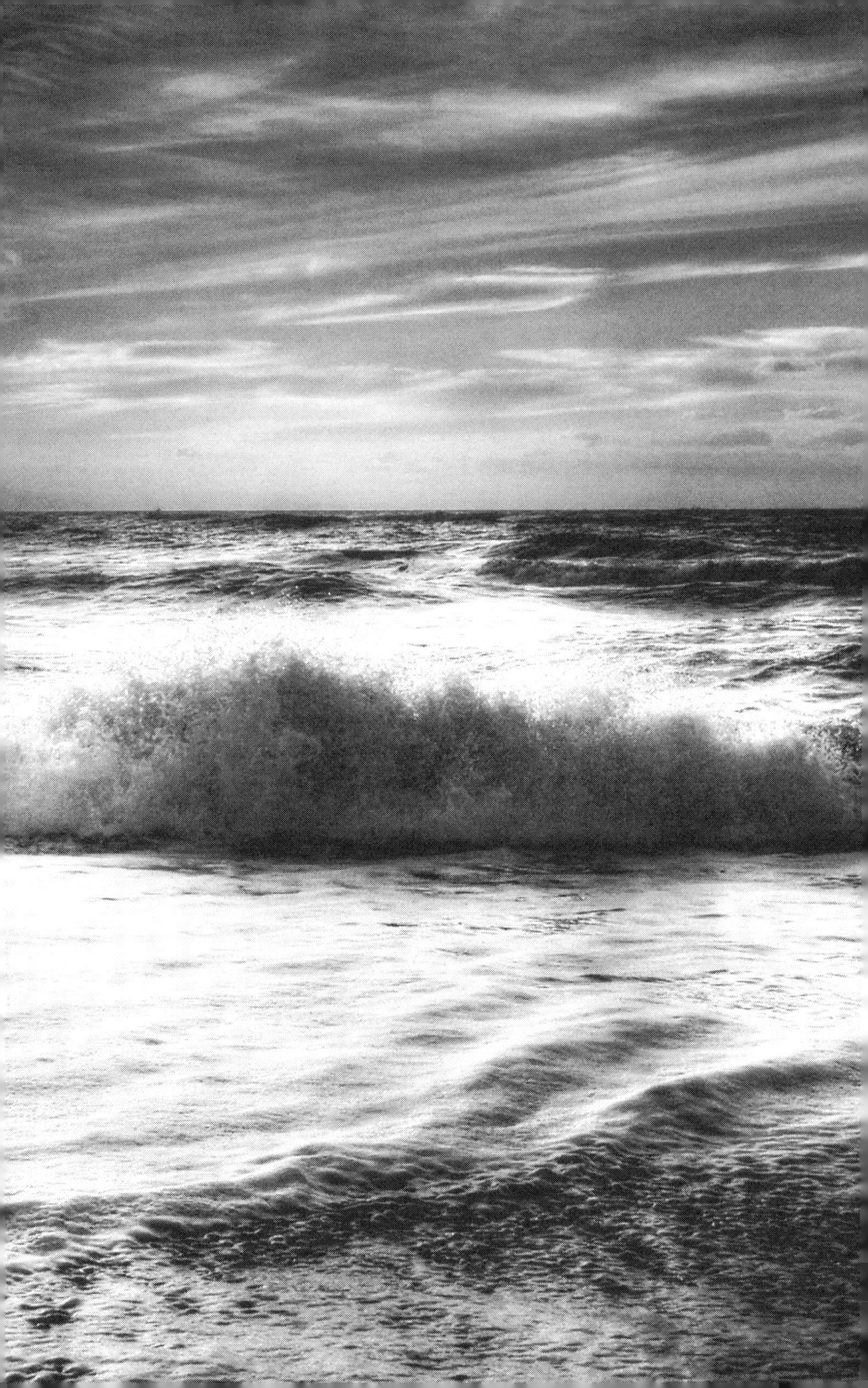

1
The Old Woman & the Sea

Erna Colebrook

Once you have reached the age of three score and ten there is the feeling that the time has come to do certain things just once more as a sort of valedictory gesture to life in all its richness.

So, when I set out with Michael, my husband, for a holiday on the north coast of Mallorca I vowed to swim one last time in that wonderfully warm and invigorating water of the Mediterranean Sea.

Many thoughts crossed my mind as I walked on the warm sand that late summer's afternoon. In ancient Greece Poseidon ruled the waves here, while Aphrodite, goddess of love (sensual and spiritual), was born from her waters, standing demurely on a scallop shell. Across this sea Rome and Carthage waged their wars. For several centuries the mercantile city of Venice held sway here. So many cultures flourished along her shores. Her creative influence has been and still is immeasurable.

My own love affair began when my parents with their four

children drove by car for two and a half days from Brussels by the old N7 to the Côte d'Azur. It was paradise for a young post-war teenager. Here the air was warm and pine scented, the cicadas were loud and persistent and the sea… Oh! the sea… the sea!

I reached the edge of the water, hesitated for a moment and stepped gently into the shallow water. My ankles didn't 'freeze up'. A good omen. I moved slowly into deeper water, step by slow step. I was up to my middle now, letting my body adjust to the colder environment. As I splashed water on my arms I realised that something odd was happening. Small fishes, dozens of them, were swimming all round me. I saw glorious silver life in a transparent sea all looking for breadcrumbs which two little girls standing at the edge were throwing into the water. Just for a moment I seemed to live in another world – a world of harmony and beingness, a world of love.

They were gone as quickly as they appeared. In high spirits I ducked into the water and had my swim.

That evening over a leisurely dinner Michael and I talked about the large painting which hangs in our living room at home. It was created by June Witheridge, a Plymouth artist. It depicts an androgynous human figure walking on the seabed accompanied by five mackerel who look quite comfortable in the presence of the stranger. There is seaweed to cope with so progress is possibly slow. All are travelling in the same direction. There is movement here, they are going somewhere together. The left arm of the human figure trails gently in the water in a gesture of caring. The head too is inclined towards the fish. Here is expressed most beautifully a gentle loving relationship, an embodiment which is not only material but for want of a better word spiritual. Here there exists, just for this moment, a communion of beings.

The painting by Plymouth artist June Witheridge.

The next day I ached all over and I was in bed with a cold. The Spanish call it 'the fruits of the season'. For them October is the season of colds.

I am not a good patient. To be confined to bed after my wonderful aquatic experience was not to my liking. Here I was, in a strange bed, in a strange room, my nose dripping. I was looking for some compassion but as there was no one about I found myself softly saying "Look at me now Julia". Instantly the face of my youngest daughter Julia appeared and then that of my mother who died three years ago. Their smiles comforted me. Life is so much about mothers. Don't dying soldiers on the battlefield call out for their mothers? It is the first bonding we make as we appear on this Earth. Then I saw my grandmother's face, and her mother's and so it went on mother after mother, generation by generation, nurturing, caring, loving and so often forgiving.

Backwards in time I seemed to travel, seeing all manner of creatures giving birth and nurturing and making sure of the next generation. I reached the point where I saw fish as my cousins, sharing a common backboned ancestor.

And beyond the planet, I travelled on to an inanimate Universe seeing stars and galaxies and their gyrations and their awe-inspiring galactic relationships. Finally, I arrived at a place of great strength and integrity. Journey's end and my destination. I saw no face but I knew instinctively that here was the abode of the Great Mother, SHE who is giving birth to the Universe, creatrix, fountain of love and forgiveness, Mother of us all. What a lineage!

To be sure all metaphors, but how else can we circumscribe

the mystery which is the Universe. Metaphors which surely resonate with our time.

I travelled full circle. I understood how each atom, each molecule from the very beginning was imbued with that quality which for lack of a better word could be called love. That the Great Epic of Evolution of the Universe did not only have a material form but also a spiritual dimension – intangible and difficult to define through scientific inquiry. From the beginning atoms, molecules and each living being possessed the capability to enter into relationship – to give of self and become a new entity, to change its environment, to be transformed again and yet again, leading to an ever more complex Universe for forms and relationships to evolve as we know them today. And this over a time span completely outside our human experience (13.7 billion years to be exact).

I understood that from the very beginning, the overriding longing to attract, to bond, to be in relationship, to search for harmony, to love and be loved, had been hardwired into the Universe project: refined by the evolutionary arrow of time. Material form cannot exist without relationship.

In our own historical time Jesus of Nazareth and his fishermen friends had a message of love for neighbour, self and enemy. Today 2000 years on, scientific and spiritual gurus are urging us to extend our love to planet Earth, for some, to Gaia. Not so easy, for a radical shift is needed. Love is not just about feelings, it is about relationships, about a way of living. New ways of organising our human lives are desperately needed at all levels of our Western culture. The exploitative conception of ourselves is looking horribly tarnished. A new longing rises up in our hearts for a more integrated way of life. We have a vision of what creative communities might look like. We perceive a new beauty (a concept dear to the native Americans). To build a different place we must give of self. We must evolve.

My chance encounter with fishes had led to unexpected disclosures. I was pleased when Michael came back from the Farmacia with the news that they don't do Lemsips here, they make them with oranges. I smiled and savoured the moment. Expect the unexpected.

* * *

Erna Colebrook is a long-standing member of GreenSpirit with a degree in zoology. She is the author of *A Spark in My Soul* and other publications with Michael Colebrook.

2
The Black Mamba*

Amelia Kinkade

Introduction by Marian Van Eyk McCain
The black mamba has a reputation for being the deadliest snake in the world, and the fastest land snake on Earth. In her book *Whispers from the Wild* (New World Library, 2016), animal communicator Amelia Kinkade tells the story of how she met one, at the African lion camp where she and her partner had been staying. Amelia had stayed there before, and although a black mamba had been seen around the camp, to her regret she had never encountered the creature. This time, however, she did, just before it was time to leave. Here, with Amelia's permission, is the story.

O n our final day we moved from an open-air hut, where anything and everything could and did crawl in from outside – primarily gargantuan insects but

---

* Editors' Note
This extract from *Whispers from the Wild* uses American spelling and punctuation from the book.

no snakes – to a proper house that had glass in the windows and doors that locked. As I was about to find out, the illusion of being in a sturdy wooden house created a false sense of security. We unpacked bags of groceries in the kitchen, thankful to be in a house that had a kitchen. Eager to explore the house, we waltzed out of the kitchen and into the living room, which was separated from the kitchen by a glass door. Jeff disappeared into the bedroom with the luggage, and I turned around, ready to come back into the kitchen to get a pop out of one of the bags. Something had called me back into the kitchen. Maybe it was more the desire for a grape soda. I looked down and noticed that one of the cabinet doors was opening…all by itself. This was a cupboard door right under where I had been standing to unpack the groceries.

What came out of this cupboard put the fear of God even in me. First her big gray head poked out of the door, and then the door opened slowly, an inch at a time. Her body started rising out of the cupboard, dancing through the air, elevated weightless in space. She was a very big snake. And as you may know, the mamba has a 'smile' painted on its face, like the Joker in Batman, and the inside of its mouth is black. So mambas are sinister looking – and rightly so, because their bite is certain death – but they also seem to be mocking you with this laughing expression just before they kill you.

I was surprised at the level of panic I felt as the adrenaline started coursing through my veins and every hair on the back of my neck stood up. She continued to move up into the air, swaying and rising. And my panic continued to escalate. Now, of course, this uncontrollable fear is against everything I teach and know to be true about the attitude to take when greeting wild animals, no matter how deadly. But for the first time in my life, I truly couldn't control my fight-or-flight instinct. It seized me completely. Fortunately, I was also captivated by her beauty, and this feeling of awe and reverence for her allowed me to keep my wits about me enough to not do something really stupid…like scream. Or run. But I had some foolish moves yet to make.

I opened the door between the living room and the kitchen very carefully, and then I tiptoed across the kitchen floor only a few feet from her and opened the kitchen door to the outside – wide open so that she could see the open air in the front yard clearly. I crept back through the kitchen and manned my watch station behind the living room door, where I hid shivering. I said to her, "There's the door. Now please leave."

I tried to remember my skills. I visualized her dropping to the floor and slithering out the door. Despite the fact that this was insanely rude of me, and the feeling behind it was the opposite of everything I teach, I was uncontrollably afraid, and I hoped she would make a quick exit. She obeyed me without question – she dropped to the floor and started sidewinding herself toward the open door. The length of her massive body was shocking, at least eight feet, and as the long, sinewy body slithered out of the cabinet, it just kept coming and coming and coming, making wide graceful S curves across the kitchen floor. She was simply massive, and in a moment of unthinkable stupidity, something in me snapped. I had a knee-jerk reaction where an old silly damsel-in-distress program kicked in. In lost-little-girl mode, I did one of the most idiotic things I've ever done in my life. I screamed for my boyfriend to come "save me." He rushed into the room, saw the colossal snake, and picked up the doormat. Then he did the stupidest thing any human could ever do. He smacked the tip of her tail with the doormat. Now, at this point, she was almost out the door – all eight feet of her. But when she felt the attack on her tail, she flew – and I do mean flew – across the room in a full-scale aerial attack.

God knows where she got the torque to do a one-eighty on the floor and hurl herself six feet in the air across the kitchen like a bolt of black lightning, targeted directly at his face. The speed of the assault was horrifying, but more shocking still was how she stopped herself mid-air just inches from his nose. She hung suspended, right in front of his pale eyes. Her body filled the length of the kitchen, but somehow she had managed to contract her body, coil back, and cut off her momentum just before her fangs reached his face. She dropped at his feet with a soft smash of pure muscle gone limp on the tile. It was the most chilling sound I'd ever heard – like a dead body falling to the floor. But no one was dead. She spared his life. Without turning around, he backed away. And she let him. She didn't strike. She whirled her head around to the direction of her safe haven in the cabinet and, in a flash, opened the cupboard door with her chin. The entire length of her body followed like a whip of melted steel. Like quicksilver, her eight-foot-long body disappeared under the kitchen sink.

Somehow I came to my senses and said to my shellshocked

boyfriend, "Please leave me alone with her. Let me handle this."

And to his credit, he did exactly that. Whether it was faith in my ability or just the uncontrollable panic that this snake instills in any human being, I don't know, but he high-tailed it out of the kitchen and left me alone with her. He and I had retreated into the living room in horror, shut the door to the kitchen, and allowed her to go right back into her hiding place. Something in me shifted, and I remembered who I was. This time I vowed to do everything right.

I opened the glass door to the kitchen. I dropped to my knees a few feet in front of the cabinet where she hid. The kitchen cabinet door was shut and the stillness in the room was eerie, as if time had stopped and life beyond this moment ceased to exist, but I'd left the door to the outside world open. I remember hearing birds chirping through that open door and seeing particles of dust whirl in the atmosphere, still electrified by her flight. I remember that the sunlight in the room was too bright, whitewashed in the presence of death, as if the gates of heaven had already opened and I had been ushered into the blinding light. There was no going back.

In my mind, I 'asked' her to come back out, while I visualized her opening the cabinet door. I knelt there for I don't know how long. I was in a slow-motion dream. Several minutes must have gone by before the door started to open again, ever so slowly. She peeked out tentatively, probably no less afraid than we were. We'd done a great job of scaring the hell out of her. Once again I saw her incredible face, and she began to lift her head right in front of my eyes, but this time I refused to see her as an evil menace. I saw her as the goddess that she was. Her graceful neck and regal head arced up until she was again showing herself, but this time meeting my gaze as I knelt in front of her. I apologized for my horrendous behavior. I told her she was indescribably beautiful, perfect in every way, and that I'd spent years wanting to meet her, but now that I was actually having that honor, I was grateful that she allowed me in her territory. I thanked her for wanting to see me, and I told her I was sorry that humans were afraid of her and failed to see her beauty.

You might not believe that black mambas can smile – what with the creepy grin already painted on their lips – but even snakes have facial expressions. I could see a change come over her face. Her eyes softened, and she danced before me, grateful for the wave of love and admiration I was emanating. You might also think I was a crazy fool to kneel four feet in front of Africa's most dangerous snake – courting death, tempting death. But if that's the case, you fail to see the point. I was already dead. I was looking death in the eye. If she had wanted to kill me, with one lightning strike I'd be dead. If I did not find a way to escort her out of the house, either my boyfriend or I, or even both of us, would most certainly be killed if one of us stumbled on her late at night.

But aside from that agenda, this meeting was important. I told her that I now knew without any question that she was indeed the queen of the black mambas and that I was sorry to have upset her, but now I was so grateful to be in her presence. I assured her that she was the most beautiful snake I'd ever seen. Then I thanked her for her benevolence and told her that I was proud of her for being so dangerous.

At this, she smiled more and danced gracefully. I admired her for a moment, an hour, an eternity – I didn't know what was happening back on earth. We were somewhere else together, in a cosmic dream where no one could hurt us, another world where we would naturally never think of hurting each other.

Eventually I dropped my focus back down into normal reality for the sake of our safety. I realized that if someone came crashing in on this sacred moment and broke our spell, she could startle and become dangerous. I suggested that when she was ready, she could drop to the floor and exit out the open door. I told her that she must be very careful to keep on moving, because if any human tripped over her, especially on the porch late at night, they might try to kill her. I visualized her slithering out the door and all the way across the porch, disappearing into the bush. I explained to her that if a human found her, she would be in great danger... I encouraged her to keep moving until she was safely out of sight from the humans.

She relished the moments of being in communion with me. We had a peaceful moment of prayer together, just admiring each other, just loving each other, being respectful for each other's ferocity – but also of each other's tenderness, joy, and hope, and the melancholy of being misunderstood. We had a moment of sharing some knowledge of injustice, of vulnerability, of being plagued by the fears, prejudices, and misperceptions of others. I told her that it was the greatest thrill of my life to get to meet her face-to-face after all these years. I knew she heard me. I could see it in her eyes. Then when she was ready, she dropped to the floor ever so softly and started crawling toward the sunlight through the open door. I didn't rush her this time. Nor did I call anyone to come rescue me. I just let her huge body slither and snake and make S curves for what seemed like forever until she found her way out of her dark hiding place and into the sunshine, safely away from the humans who could do her harm. Would that we all find our way into the sunshine.

* * *

Amelia Kinkade was born in Fort Worth, Texas, is an actress, animal communicator and author of several books on animal communication.

3
Earth Activist Training, Permaculture, & Simple Techniques for Saving the World!

Jonathan Furst

For the first time in a very long time, I have hope. Hope that we can make it. That it is possible to clean up toxic waste. To re-green our damaged planet. To halt the cycles of war and exploitation. To provide abundance in just a few acres per person, and restore the majority of land back to the wild. This is not just hope, but certain knowledge. We can do it with the technology we have, with the resources we've got. I know because I've seen it with my own eyes, done it with my own hands. I know, because I went to Earth Activist Training.

Crash Course in Planetary Survival
For two weeks, Starhawk and Penny Livingston-Stark led fifty

people to learn, live, and practise skills for ecological living and magical activism. Kind of a "Save the World 101". What it comes down to is Permaculture – an outlook and method for working with Nature's processes, rather than against. It's not just about growing large amounts of food on little land; it's about building houses for $500 or less, redesigning urban environments, restoring damaged lands, and living on the planet in harmony. It's a huge leap beyond simple sustainability. It's about giving more back to the planet than we take out. And that's what humans are good at. I know it might not seem like that's true – most of the time it feels like all we really do is create war, suffering, and destruction. We do still live under the shadows of pollution and the bomb. Still on the brink of killing off not just ourselves, but all life on Earth. But that's only half of the story. For example, did you know in Nature it takes about 100 years to create a quarter inch of topsoil? But in a compost heap, humans can help create a full inch of soil in just four years. We're natural soil-builders. If we have an evolutionary niche, it's to work with the worms, fungi, and other little life-makers – and we're phenomenally successful at it. Look at China, where they've been doing it religiously for thousands of years.

Enhancing natural processes is our biological right and our inheritance. When Penny explained that, I felt like she'd given me back a piece of my soul. Right after that, she and Starhawk took us outside and showed us how to put a compost pile together. We got in there with our shovels and pitchforks. We piled manure on straw, layered on buckets of kitchen scraps, and finally brought in those wonderful worms.

Then – this is a key piece – we left the pile to do its own thing. "If you have a choice between two equally good options", our teachers advised, "and one takes less work than the other, always choose the one with less work". You can turn and fuss with a pile a whole lot. But if you set it up right, you can just walk away – heck, you can even plant your crops right in the compost pile – and only deal with it when you're adding more material. That's a major principle of Permaculture: minimum effort for maximum return. To put it another way, life demands we conserve as much energy as possible. And that means setting up self-perpetuating, synergistic systems that work with Nature ('weeds', 'pests', and other 'nuisances') rather than trying to eradicate them. In one example, we saw video footage of a Permaculture site that had been untended for several years. Left to its own devices, the garden had developed into an Eden of fruits and vegetables, without human guidance or interference.

Structure and Spirit

The workshop was a non-stop, total immersion course in options. After an early breakfast, we'd gather and cast a circle for the day – playing games, grounding, singing, and invoking the directions. Then off to the first of three, three-hour sessions (usually two lectures and one hands-on) plus affinity group gardening, Permaculture design group projects, and individual offerings from other students in the course. Daily themes were divided by elements – Earth: natural building, gardening, and how to finance the land you live on; Air: wind power, design process, and global climate; Water:

water harvesting, roof catchments, global politics, greywater and remediation; Fire: renewable energy, biodiesel, and direct action; and so on.

Without the morning's spiritual foundation (plus Witchcraft mini-lessons throughout the day) we could easily have become exhausted by the pace. But most days I felt invigorated rather than overwhelmed. The hands-on activities really helped, too. Actually digging earthworks and building greywater systems took the knowledge out of our heads and planted it firmly in our bodies. The work was hard, but when you're planting trees or digging swales (strategic ditches for erosion control and remediating the water table) with the intention of working with Nature it feels a whole lot different than doing chores in your parents' backyard. In fact, I was often struck by how counterproductive much of the yard work I'd done as a kid had been. So many weekends my parents had me digging up dandelions and other 'weeds' that we could have eaten, raking and tossing leaves that would have provided excellent ground cover, and spraying noxious chemicals that probably seeped into the water table long ago. How much easier if we'd simply let the trees mulch themselves, rather than spend all that effort and money trying to manage Nature.

Working with and for the Earth can take a host of forms; most days we'd have guest instructors, bringing a variety of views and knowledge. Hilary McQuie (of the RANT activist training collective) and her partner, Mike Dolan (Green Party organiser), discussed grassroots organising from the anarchic global justice and traditional political models. Joe Kennedy from Builders Without Borders taught us cob construction and other low-cost housing options. Folks from the Occidental Arts and Ecology Center showed us how to look at the land from a Permaculture design standpoint, taught us a history of the rise of corporations and resources for curbing their power, gave us the tools to set up land trusts and other financing options, and discussed group process and how to live in community.

The first few days were a little difficult, as many of the lessons focused on discussing the full extent of the world's political, economic, and ecological challenges. You've got to know what you're dealing with before you can start to fix it, but the sheer load of information had many of us on the edge of despair. Luckily, we were also learning the elements of magical activism – grounding, nonviolent action, how to cast a circle, how to ground while moving, how to read each other's energy patterns, and a host of other skills for nourishing ourselves while standing up to power. There was an amazing water trance, where we envisioned ourselves as a pure drop of water, rising to the clouds, falling to earth, joining other drops in a torrent from stream to ocean and back to our unique selves. Lisa Fithian (long-time activist and EAT co-student) led several nonviolent trainings and simulations, and also gave us an inspiring history of the Global Justice movement. We also discussed trauma and how to heal from the perils of activism, from physical violence to emotional exhaustion. Spirit sustained us throughout the course. My companions came from a wide variety of locations and cultures, including activists from India, Croatia, Montana, and the Pomo nation. Some identified as Pagans, others as Christians, Hindus, Jews,

Atheists, or Seekers. Given this variety of backgrounds, the techniques we learned were introductory. But the lessons ran deep as we applied them directly to the tasks at hand. The lessons were also pretty much dogma-free (beyond a basic love for the Earth), making magic accessible to everyone in the class.

Making It Real

I try to live simply, consuming about half the resources of the average American. So I was shocked to find out that in order to exist at what I consider a sustainable level, I'd need to reduce my consumption by over five times. As one presenter pointed out, that's a lot more than recycling a few more cans. It means that if we – and almost every species on Earth – are to survive, we need to radically, fundamentally change the way we do things. When I tell this to my friends, many become depressed. "It's hopeless", they say, "we'll never make it". But I found the information inspiring. To me, it's a complete validation of the work we do. It's an impetus, an imperative from the Earth that we go farther than we ever imagined. Now is not the time for half measures – take your wildest fantasy and go for it! There is no other way to survive.

That's the real lesson of Earth Activist Training. Dream big, then go out and make it happen. Not just because it's fun and it's the right thing to do. We have to. There's no waiting around for technology to save us. In fact, all the technology we need is right here, right now. Not just pipes, and systems, and theories. But spirit, and magic, and most of all, hope. Go to EAT (or almost any Permaculture course) and you'll learn enough to grasp the world's challenges and the web of interconnected options for solving them. You'll be overwhelmed with options, but one will call out, "This is what I can do, and here's how I can start".

For me, I decided that my goal is to reduce my consumption to less than zero – to give more to Earth than I take out. If I can do that one thing with my life, it will be a success. If I learn how and pass it on to others, I can be part of the miracle. So can you. If you feel alone, if you doubt there's hope for us as a species, take heart. The options are out there right now. I know. I've lived the possibilities. You can, too. It's a beautiful future, just waiting for us to make it happen.

* * *

Jonathan Furst: Earth Activist Training really did change Jonathan's life. Shortly after completing his course in 2002, he quit his day job to go live in the forests of Mendocino, where he wrote this article. Today, he is a professional Naturalist & Nature Connection instructor, a Reclaiming teacher, and the Maggid (Jewish spiritual facilitator/storyteller) for Keneset HaLev in San Francisco. You can contact him at: jfurst@pobox.com

PART TWO

BALANCE & HEALING

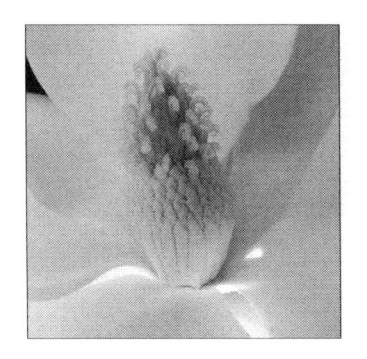

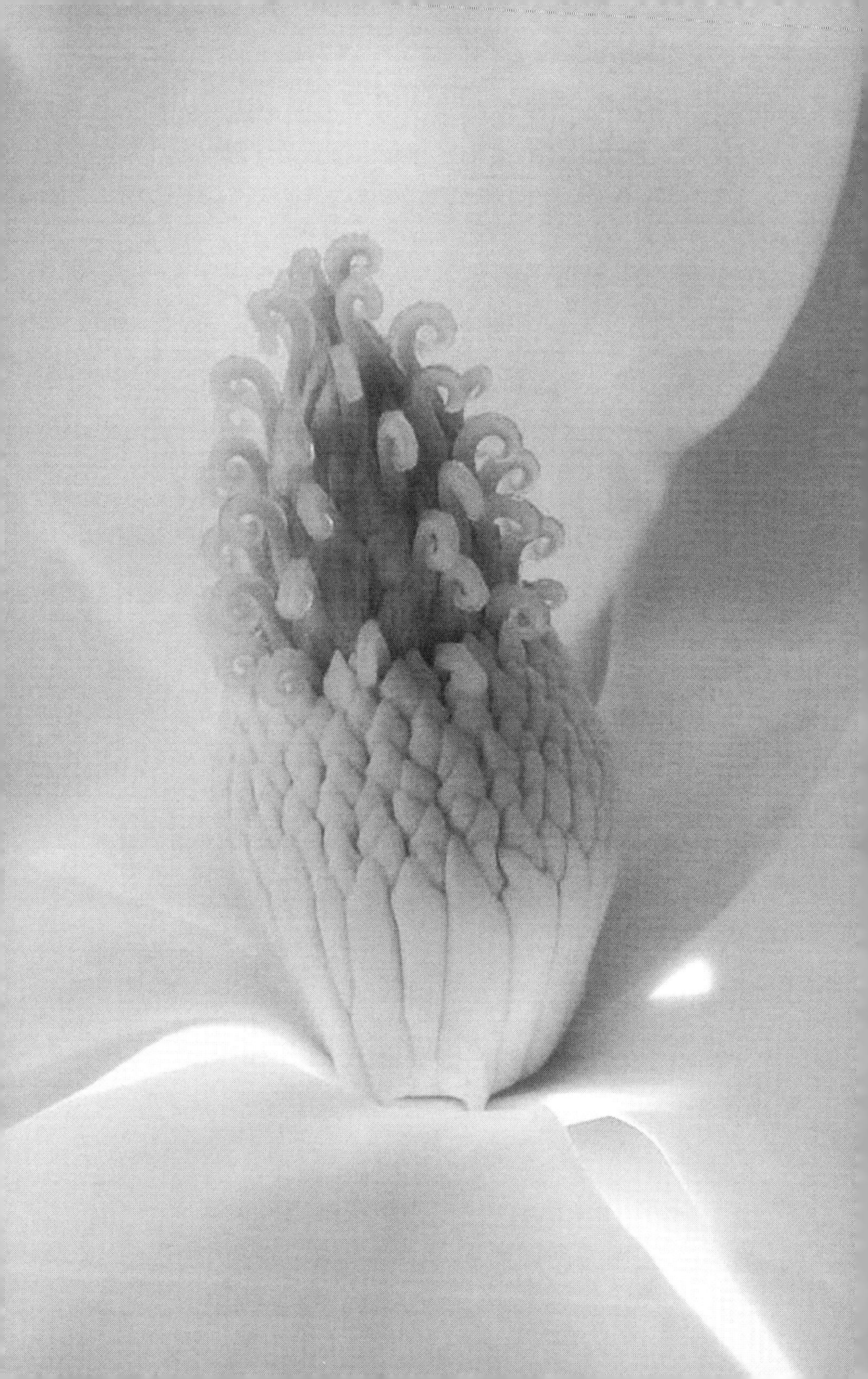

4
Living on the Edge
A View Through the Lens of Complexity

Jean Boulton

On the edges of ecosystems, things never quite settle down. If you took snapshots of the flora and fauna on the edge of a forest over several years, you would see the woodland encroaching a little on the surrounding grassland and then pulling back. You would see grassland plants on the edges of the forest and forest species creeping into the woodland and the associated insects and mammals from 'either side' would, in the same way, be present in this zone of transition. In technical terms, the variation and fluctuating environment means that the ecosystem never becomes efficient, never optimises, never quite settles to definite ecological pathways and unambiguous patterns of relationships. This is because the conditions keep changing.

This diversity in these transition regions, at these edges, spawns resilience. The ecosystems are able to adapt to changing circumstances because it is the changing circumstances that have shaped them. Varying conditions lead to variety in ecological relationships, provide more than one option for what to eat or where to live.

This description of life at the edge is to be contrasted with what happens in very stable ecosystems. Chris Holling's (2002) observations of forests make this very clear. He says:

> *Over time as the forest matures and passes into the late part of its growth phase … species and organisms are progressively more specialized and efficient in using the energy and nutrients available in their niche. Indeed, the whole forest becomes extremely efficient … In the process, redundancies in the forest's ecological network … are pruned away. New plants and animals find fewer niches to exploit, so the steady increase in diversity of species and organisms slows and may even decline.*

He goes on to say:

> *The forest's ever-greater connectedness and efficiency eventually produce diminishing returns by reducing its capacity to cope with severe outside shocks. Essentially, the ecosystem becomes less resilient. The forest's interdependent trees, worms, beetles, and the like become so well adapted to a specific range of circumstances – and so well organized as an efficient and productive system – that when a shock pushes the forest far outside that range, it can't cope. Also, the forest's high connectedness helps any shock travel faster across the ecosystem … Overall, then, the forest ecosystem becomes rigid and brittle.*

So Holling shows us that over time and in stable conditions, Nature itself becomes more efficient and rigid and as a result cannot respond to shocks or change. This presents a dilemma. In Australia, for example – as described by Flattery (1994) in his interesting book *The Future Eaters* – the poorness of the conditions, the difficulty in surviving at all, means that species become very specialised. One type of reed, for example, might have one beetle living at its top, another species near the middle and another near the base. They have become very adapted to conditions that are poor but stable and created very narrow niches. In similar vein, one type of bird flies to one particular lake for a few days at one particular time of the year to breed. And (the example I like best) the koala has in fact evolved to have a brain smaller than its brain capacity in order to use less energy, live on a poor diet. (As an aside, this is a great example of how evolution can lead to *less* sophistication, *less* complexity. Evolution is about adapting to prevailing conditions not 'ascending the great chain of being' as used to be thought.)

So the point here is that specialisation can sometimes lead to survival where, otherwise, survival would be impossible. So specialisation is not all bad! There is a trade-off between the efficiency of specialisation and the resilience of diversity.

What does this all imply for societies, for organisations and for us as individuals trying to live well, trying to live in harmony with the planet? What is the balance between resilience and efficiency, between working effectively with 'the now' and being poised to adapt to 'the future'?

First of all, it is interesting to note that the trend to less diversity, to less resilience, to greater connectivity is a natural process as exemplified by Holling's work on forests. We see the same trend in, say, the finance sector. If left to itself, the ecology of the finance sector demonstrably leads to few, big banks, intricately interconnected. It moves away from 'the edge'. The process of the big getting bigger and the powerful getting more powerful (Boulton 2010) is due to positive feedback (or increasing returns as the economists call it). And it is very interesting to recognise that ecologies can get 'locked in', become hard to shift when they have got their grip. Mature forests are hard to penetrate with new species. And forests in this situation are not resilient to shocks and tend to collapse if there is a fire or a shift in the climate. Similarly, sectors of society or sectors of commerce, if they become too powerful, become hard to modify, hard to oppose or change. And yet they are also at risk of collapse, as we have seen with the banks and may yet see again.

So this thinking suggests that there needs to be some balancing factors, some regulation (as there used to be in the UK finance sector until 1989), some social rules that counter this trend, that represent the less powerful and represent the voice of the future and of the planet. To argue that we need some regulatory processes of course stands against the argument that the market will sort this out, will give freedom of choice and empower the consumer. Cambridge economist Ha-Joon Chang (2011), in his well-worth-reading book, *23 Things They Don't Tell You about Capitalism*, supports this view and also makes the point that in practice no markets are entirely 'free' anyway. For example, in the West, we regulate against child labour. We regard this as so 'normal' that we don't see it as regulation. But in certain countries where there are no such restrictions, child labour is common and, as comes to light, some Western High Street brands seem prepared to exploit this regulatory gap. The same argument can be used regarding the sale of cigarettes to children in developing countries, making construction sites safe for workers, controlling pollution. Regulatory processes have a role to play in mediating the short-term profit focus of commerce. And where such regulation does not exist, the 'freer market' can indeed, it seems, lead to exploitation of the weak and increased profit to the powerful. (Since the adoption of neo-liberal free market policies the difference in the US between the salaries of workers and those of CEOs of the top companies has move from 20-to-1 in the 1960s to 250-to-1 in 2006 (The Economist, 2012).

So, to keep the commercial sector from 'locking-in', becoming unassailable, we need to question free-market ideology at its extreme. Regulation – formal, or informal through public pressure and social movements – has a role to play in moving us back towards 'the edge', to a position of greater diversity and resilience, where the voices and rights of the less powerful, where consideration of the planet and of the future are still in the mix.

What about life 'on the edge' for an organisation? This idea of living on the edge has been translated into the notion of living on the 'edge of chaos' (Waldrop 1992). Are organisations more effective if they find a position between too few routines and too much bureaucracy? Can they, as Maclean and MacIntosh (2011) investigated, exhibit *spontaneous, prolific, complex and continuous change.* They undertook research with 18 organisations to find out. Of the 18, they found only two who could be considered as 'on the edge' and both these were pinned there by senior managers who kept changing the rules, creating ambiguity, shifting people in their roles. They concluded that "there was no evidence that the adoption of these practices improved the performance of the company".

So what can we conclude from this? Perhaps that getting from rigidity to fluidity cannot effectively be achieved by merely meddling from above. Indeed changing the culture of bureaucratic organisations is well-recognised as being extremely problematic. Even when organisations decentralise, and really act to empower teams and allow flexibility, the long hand of the past (and the shorter hand of those who may lose power in the process) can still be felt. The ideal is not to become rigid in the first place, but to be vigilant, to take corrective action as it happens. And this needs a wide perspective, a willingness not to concentrate power and a new mindset. To move rigid organisations towards the edge is the holy grail for organisation consultants and change managers.

Finally, how about life 'on the edge' for an individual? I've had reason to reflect on this from my own recent experience. This summer, my Mother, who lives in Yorkshire, was not expected to survive more than a few weeks. In parallel, I had sold my house in Bath. I ended up moving to Yorkshire, living in her house and engaging with the complexities of the NHS. I had left my home, my friends, my routines. Most of my worldly goods were in store. My Mother was fading away. I had little practical or emotional support where I was living. I did not recognise at the time just how 'over the edge' I felt. It started to show up as emotionality, inability to make decisions, poor concentration. Every action seemed to require a long-drawn out analysis, every grimace in every interaction seemed filled with meaning. I was on the brink of a descent into the choppy waters of chaos.

So this is the thing about living with uncertainty, with diversity, with multiple options. Too much can be debilitating; too little can lead to rigidity, to an inability to seize opportunities, to experiment, to see things from other angles. I can see I need some parts of my life, some parts of my frame of reference, to be stable enough to allow room to manoeuvre in other parts. If I make myself too comfortable, flee too much from anxiety, I stop questioning my beliefs or my behaviours, stop engaging in the wider world of opportunities and uncertainties. If I throw myself to too great a degree into the unknown, I run the risk of becoming ineffective and lost.

So, living on the edge is paradoxical, not straightforward. Too much can lead to chaos; too little can lead to rigidity and risk of collapse. And how do we know when is enough and when is too much? We – and organisations and societies – cannot move too quickly, cannot be changed overnight by dictat because the structures that have already evolved still shape our responses. We, individually and collectively, need to creep towards the edge, be uncertain about the path and the destination, try things out, peer into the shadow and continue to live with questions not answers. Where the edge is and how to get there and how to stay there when you do are questions that do not have answers. To quote Rilke:

I would like to beg you ... to love the questions themselves as if they were locked rooms or books written in a very foreign language. Don't search for the answers ... Live the questions now. Perhaps then, someday far in the future, you will gradually, without even noticing it, live your way into the answer.

References

Are They Worth It? The Economist, 2012.
Boulton, J. *Complexity Theory and Implications for Policy Development.* Emergence: Complexity and Organisation 12:2, p.31–41, 2010.
Chang, H-J. *23 Things They Don't Tell You about Capitalism*, Penguin, 2011.
Flattery, T. *The Future Eaters*, New York, Grove Press, 1994.
Holling, CS. *Panarchy: Understanding Transformations in Human and Natural Systems*, Island Press, 2002.
MacLean, D, and MacIntosh, R. *Organizing at the Edge of Chaos: Insights from Action Research*, in *The SAGE Handbook of Complexity and Management*, P Allen, S Maguire, and B McKelvey. Sage, 2011.
Waldrop, MM. *Complexity*, Simon and Schuster, 1992.

* * *

Jean Boulton is a strategy consultant and part-time academic at both Bath and Cranfield universities. She researches, teaches, consults, and writes about the implications of complexity thinking for strategy, management and policy development. She has been a non-executive director and trustee and senior manager for a number of organisations. She is a Fellow of the Institute of Physics. She has a keen interest in Buddhism and Daoism and in the interdependencies and overlaps between science and spirituality. She is first author of *Embracing Complexity*, published in 2015, by OUP.

5
Healing Our Cities

Marian Van Eyk McCain

When I interviewed Druid writer Emma Restall Orr for GreenSpirit magazine some years ago,[1] I asked her how she thought city dwellers could best stay in touch with Nature when they were surrounded by concrete. Emma replied:

> *We can honour nonhuman nature, nurturing it within the concrete jungles of our planet, but each day we must also ... find the currents in the city, the forces and flows, the eddies and tides ... of crowds and traffic, in human noises, human creativity, human interaction, emotions, colours and energies. Nothing is negative or inherently evil, there is potential inspiration, positivity, in everything. Our task is to find the current, feeling how we are a part of it, how we might influence it, bringing joy and wakefulness to its flow.*

For a Nature-lover, whose heart can so easily feel uplifted by a walk through the woods, there might appear to be little inspiration in the cement and glass canyons of the city. Yet

Manhattan, the part of New York City with the deepest of those canyons, has such a vibrant current of life running through it that on first impact it almost knocks you over. New Yorkers surf that energy wave and they love it. So what is this quality? Why do some places have it while others don't? Why do some areas feel vibrantly alive and others cold and dead?

According to architect Christopher Alexander:

There is a central quality which is the root criterion of life and spirit in a man, a town, a building, or a wilderness. This quality is objective and precise, but it cannot be named.

He explains that any building, any town, any place is made not only out of the physical ingredients that compose it but the patterns of movements and events, the flow of energy in and around it, and particularly those that are repetitive:

The specific patterns out of which a building or town is made may be alive or dead... The more living patterns there are in a place ... the more it glows ... the more it has that self-maintaining fire which is the quality without a name ... then it becomes a part of nature, like ocean waves or blades of grass, its parts are governed by the endless play of repetition and variety created in the presence of the fact that all things pass.[2]

To Alexander, the art and skill of good architecture depend on recognising and understanding this nameless quality of aliveness and proceeding accordingly:

When you build a thing, you cannot merely build that thing in isolation, but must also repair the world around it, and within it, so that the larger world at that one place becomes more coherent, and more whole, and the thing which you make takes its place in the web of nature, as you make it.[3]

It has been his life's work to teach others how to shape their bricks-and-mortar creations to take their place in that web of Nature and to bring balance, harmony and health to the people who use them.

Of course it is not a new idea. This wisdom has been around for six millennia in the East, where *Feng shui* is a widely accepted and widely followed discipline. *Feng shui* is the subtle art of placement, of creating and aligning elements in order to optimise the flow of the invisible energy known as *chi* or *ki* in the East and *prāna* in India. Modern Druids call it *nwyfre*. Most of us don't have a name for it but our souls and bodies recognise it nonetheless. Unfortunately, most urban spaces and buildings in the West are designed and built with no sensitivity whatsoever to these subtle energy currents and as a consequence they can drain or tire us rather than nurturing us, though we may not realise why.

So what to do? We cannot tear our cities down and rebuild them. What we can do, according to Jaime Lerner, whose new book *Urban Acupuncture*[4] was published late last year, is to find ways of bringing life back into dead spaces and restoring the flow of energy to places where it has been blocked or stifled.

Lerner, who was three times mayor of Curitiba, Brazil, and is also an architect and a popular advocate for sustainable and liveable urbanism, describes how some city planners have worked to restore life and dynamism to ailing urban areas. Sometimes remedies might be large and bold, such as the disinterring of a neglected, sewer-like watercourse in Seoul, Korea, that had been paved over to make a road and turning it into a living, vibrant river, edged with plantings and pedestrian walkways. New York and Paris did something similar when they repurposed old, disused railway lines as linear urban parks, creating delightful new energy flows. Several large American cities such as San Francisco have deconstructed downtown freeways, with great results.

Other interventions such as establishing farmers' markets and co-ops and turning old factories into shopping centres have relied more on people than on bulldozers. But in every case, the object has been to restore those mysterious currents of aliveness that we find healthy, comforting and pleasant and which help to bring us together and deepen our connections with each other and with the habitat that sustains us. This is why Lerner likens this work to acupuncture, calling it 'pinpricks' of urbanism projects, people, and initiatives that ripple through their communities to uplift city life. He says:

> *I believe that some of the magic of medicine can and should be applied to cities, for many of them are ailing and some are almost terminal. Just as good medicine depends on the interaction between doctor and patient, successful urban planning involves triggering healthy responses within the city, probing here and there to stimulate improvements and positive chain reactions.*

Intervention is all about revitalization, an indispensable way of making an organism function and change.

In urban health, just as in rural health, diversity is a key element. Vast tracts of car-based suburbia are to the city what monocultures are to the countryside. As Lerner points out:

A city pocked with lifeless suburbs or tracts of urban real estate devoid of housing is just as skewed as one strewn with abandoned lots and ramshackle buildings. Filling up these many urban 'voids' can be the first step to sound acupuncture. An important step is to add elements that may be missing from a given area. If there is plenty of commerce or industry but no people, then housing development could be encouraged. If another district is all homes and apartment blocks, why not boost services? And if a building is crumbling or a shop closes its doors, something new must be built in its place even if it's only temporary ... any initiative must be taken quickly, so as not to break the continuity of urban life. Continuity IS life.

The publishers of *Urban Acupuncture* describe it as "a love letter to the elements that make a street hum with life or a neighbourhood feel like home." After all, when you love your home you take care of it and it, in turn, takes care of you. The health of the environment is as important in the city as it is anywhere else, and with more and more people living in cities, urban good health is of ever-increasing importance to the health of the planet. Parks, community gardens, piazzas with outdoor tables and strolling musicians, lakes and streams and tree-lined boulevards, archways and alleyways, areas with perfectly placed sculptures, half hidden courtyards with glimpses of flowers, a bench with a view of the river – these are all places where healthy energy tends to flow. These are places that draw us, nourish us and help us stay spiritually healthy.

It may be the smell of coffee and croissants that draws us towards coffee shops but it is not only that and the free wi-fi which tempt us to linger there. It is also the presence of that indefinable, super-comfortable something that the Scandinavians call *hygge* and the Dutch call *gezellig*. Our English language has no word for it and yet, like everybody else, we recognise it and are drawn to it. Like any other creature, when our habitat feels cosily 'just right' to us we humans smile and relax and our hearts open. People like those I have quoted here understand the vital importance of that for the health of individuals and communities.

Crime, violence, vandalism, alienation, these are the most obvious symptoms of urban sickness. But there are lesser, more subtle symptoms too, such as the stress and weariness that comes from too much exposure to crowds and traffic and the soullessness of so many of our public spaces. To heal these symptoms, both great and small, we must pay more attention to energy flows and how best to channel them for the healing of our cities and ourselves.

References

1. GreenSpirit magazine, Summer 2008, 10:2.
2. Alexander, C. *The Timeless Way of Building*, OUP, 1980.
3. Alexander, C. *A Pattern Language*, OUP, 1978.
4. Lerner, J. *Urban Acupuncture*, Island Press, 2014.

* * *

Marian Van Eyk McCain, a retired psychotherapist, is co-editor of GreenSpirit magazine, a columnist, and author of five non-fiction books, a novel and a short story collection. She writes on green spirituality, wellness (both personal and planetary), conscious aging, ecopsychology, and green, simple living and has also published poetry and book reviews and edited the anthology *GreenSpirit: Path to a New Consciousness* (Earth Books, 2010).

6
The Healing Garden
A Personal Tribute to the Work of Pioneering Transpersonal Therapist Jenny Grut (1955 – 2006)

Richard Adams

People who are deprived of contact with the natural world suffer psychological damage.

If we do not consider ourselves connected with nature we are in a state of disconnection ...
— JENNY GRUT

Jenny Grut was a trained psychotherapist who worked for the Medical Foundation for the care of victims of torture. Born in Argentina, she had an artistic bent and found herself working with film makers in Buenos Aires. This was the time of the military junta and she witnessed first-hand the brutal suppression of freedom of expression. Finding herself at risk – friends and colleagues were being 'disappeared' – she escaped to London and worked in commercial animation and as a language translator. While in London she met therapist and human rights worker Helen Bamber OBE. Helen worked with survivors of the holocaust in Bergen Belsen. Many years later she became director of the Medical Foundation (since renamed Freedom from torture) and Jenny, inspired by her work, trained as a psychotherapist. In 1992 Helen supported the setting up of the Natural Growth Project (NGP) within the Medical foundation as a service for victims of political violence or torture. Jenny contacted me as a medical herbalist to help with this project; we met, fell in love and married.

The Natural Growth Project

Jenny founded the NGP on the idea that a person who has experienced profound loss can regain their sense of wholeness by making a connection with their natural environment. She saw Nature as a medium of communication and wanted to take the psychotherapeutic encounter out of the consultation room and into the Project's allotments. In so doing she demonstrated how this new setting facilitated non-verbal communication, a dimension that proved so valuable with clients who often had English as a second language and/or experience of severe trauma in office like rooms.

In 1996 Jenny was generously offered a house and gardens in West Hampstead, London. This allowed the NGP to develop its client base to those too physically unwell to work on allotments. Its users named it the 'Remembrance Garden'. Now Jenny had the vehicle to develop her one to one and group therapy in a unique client centred setting that was taking it beyond horticultural therapy. She was beginning a way of working with clients that would become known as 'ecotherapy'. Her vision was to move therapeutic work in a garden beyond the mentally and physically incapable to a wider population suffering from mental or physical trauma and to use gardening activities as tools for transforming the psyche. Helen recognised this innovatory work in her Preface to Jenny's book *The Healing Fields*:

> *I know of no other project which embraces the lessons of nature combined with the skills and discipline of psychotherapeutic principles. It is difficult to find adequate words to describe what is an inspiring and profound project.*

How the Natural Growth Project was Set Up
Jenny developed a team approach. She thought it better to work in supportive therapeutic pairs, psychotherapist/gardener or psychotherapist/psychotherapist, particularly with those suffering from flashbacks as in post-traumatic stress disorders. The therapeutic aim was to help clients regain their sense of self and to integrate their internal trauma. Jenny thought it important to encourage a reciprocal response to plants as she found it fostered nurturing and supportive attitudes.

She observed that gardening in a group or with a supporting team helped clients to reach into themselves and reach out to others who had suffered similar abuse. The group gardening activities helped to diffuse the sense of isolation, painfully present, in those who had been imprisoned. It helped them to rediscover and restore their social selves and their ability to see a future and plan for it, as one needs to do if you are to cultivate herbs or vegetables. It also helped them to express powerful emotions, like grief and anger while maintaining a sense of security in yourself and the group; learn new skills; adjust to a changed environment; reawaken self confidence and trust; value and reward yourself, as when you eat your produce in the due season. The NGP was to provide a crucible where clients could transform loss into gain, despair into hope, hope into confidence, death into life.

Nature as Teacher

One of Jenny's Iranian clients tells of his connection with Nature via a view of a tall tree from a prison cell:

> *If it was winter or summer, cold or hot, storm or breeze, my tree taught me all the news with absolute silence ... I would imagine myself being a bird, flying around, diving into the heart of the sky, feeling the fresh air, my body, flying higher and higher, seeing the colours of mountains and fields, looking at the children playing and chasing each other ... All these thoughts gave me a reason to stay alive.*

Jenny thought of Nature as a teacher: "I believe that we are part of nature and that if we study and observe nature we will see the ways in which it can get incredible knocks and diseases, yet regenerates. There is a sort of inner core that will regenerate." The therapeutic encounters were always written up and well structured. Firstly, she met and found out about the client's story and asked how they thought she might help them. She asked them about their symptoms and started to plan the client's gardening work depending on their physical and psychic state. Once the contact with Nature began Jenny thought "the inner landscape starts to accompany the outer landscape". Over time the traumatic story emerges to inform the client and therapist. In this unfolding she would observe and mirror back what took place to help the client engage in their own process. She found that clients quickly contacted moments of trauma so they could be worked with. To Jenny Nature was more than just a setting in which to do therapy; it was an active third force that was even more important than the therapist.

This Garden is for Healing, Not for Show: The Story of the Healing Garden and the Butterfly Woman

The Butterfly woman (BW) a client who is working in the remembrance garden bends over the densely shrubbed bed that needs thinning. Jenny says, "Have to find a nice new home for them ... after all we don't want the same thing to happen to them as happened to you".

BW tugs a large shrub and it resists. She fetches a spade and pushes it down with all her strength. The shrub keels over. BW heaves and hurls it into the air triumphantly. Then the next shrub, up it must come out of here! And the next one and the next one. "There's no place for you here anymore; we have to get you out of here! Do you want to be trapped? Can't you hear the planes? They're coming back. Hurry! grab what you can run with, got to get out of here, yes that's right run we've got to go faster away from the flames, faster, watch out for that building it might collapse any moment, Oh my God! they are right behind us. The noise is like thunder droning louder and louder, the sky is black with them. We must get out of here we must get…"

BW hears Jenny calling her name. "Are you alright? Can you hear me? Do you know what has happened?" Jenny speaks gently.

She starts to remember. They had been talking about clearing a space for her in the flower bed. They had been talking about her mother's garden back home. As a young girl she had fashioned a butterfly out of pebbles which she had painted with different bright colours. Jenny had suggested that she might like to recreate the butterfly here. Jenny had said that she needed to find a new home for the shrubs. Jenny had said she knew that BW understood what it was like to be forcibly removed from one's home.

This encounter had created a direct link back to BW's own transplantation and she began wreaking the same damage on the garden that had been done to her. Over the next few weeks BW, Jenny and the Gardener prepare together for the new butterfly. It emerged with double wings all the better to fly with and its outline was to be made with medicinal herbs linked to her physical and psychological ailments. Some herbs would be from her homeland and some from her adopted country England.

In time the butterfly is completed and Jenny asks BW to inscribe a word beneath it that will heal her. "Salaam" she says.

"But we have visitors to our garden from many different countries so perhaps you can find an English word that everyone can understand", Jenny asks.

"Salaam means peace."

Peace is a good word to use, they both agree.

BW takes her herb teas and oils that she has well researched for her headaches, monthly cramps, stomach aches, anxiety, and sleeplessness. They all fade away as she heals herself with the herbs. She asks the gardener to help her cultivate another area of the garden to grow herbs for others who have ailments like hers.

Jenny contacts some medical herbalists, for guidance on safe and effective herbs and their processing. The Healing Garden is born filled with herbs and BW's herbal tea clinic for fellow sufferers was to follow. I became a voluntary supervisor.

The day came when BW no longer needed the Healing Garden. She bade farewell to the butterfly, handed over the labelled jars and drying herbs to her successor in the herb clinic and stepped back into the world.

I Remember Standing next to Jenny…

At various fundraising events or promoting her NGP with journalists the question which is at once obvious and profound always arrived – "What is it that you do and how does it work?" It wasn't easy to answer then and it isn't easy to answer now. Jenny would say something like, "The work uses words but is beyond words. For without words an unheard language emerges that can only be listened to when the self is awakened". One day, I was with her on the north

London allotments working with victims of torture from Saddam's Iraq. A woman told me, "Your wife, Richard, for me she is like an angel working in this hospital, the hospital with the blue sky I call it". You had to witness the client's facial expression, her eyes, and the opening gesture of her arms gazing upwards while having her feet rooted in the earth of the vegetable patch to begin to grasp the meaning of this work. Jenny told me, "It all comes together in the smile". The smile, she thought, clearly signals a person who is functioning psychosocially and has hope for the future. I smile now to think of the many engaging conversations over a glass of wine into the small hours of the night knowing that we shared a belief that reconnecting with Nature and using plants can repair shattered minds and bodies. We agreed on four words that informed both of us about our work: 'remembering, in Nature, heals'.

As Jenny, wrote in her book *The Healing Fields*:

From my observations people who have difficulty in relating to other people seem to find it easier to caress a leaf, smell a flower, talk to a bird, and once this is established and they feel safe they can move on to people. Concentration, physical exercise, peaceful sounds and open spaces seem to help break down psychological defences and allow their more vulnerable, hurt or angry aspects to emerge. There is no need to present a persona in this non-human world of green, brown and blue.

References

Extracts from *The Healing Fields*, Grut, J, and Linden, S (2002). By kind permission of the publishers, Francis Lincoln, London.

Natural Growth Project Today

Freedom from Torture's Natural Growth Project combines horticulture and psychotherapy, taking as its fundamental premise that everyone, everywhere, whatever their experiences, has a continuing relationship with Nature. www.freedomfromtorture.org

Freedom from Torture

Freedom from Torture provides survivors of torture and their families with medical and social care, practical assistance and psychological and physical therapies. Freedom from Torture, Tel: 020 7697 7777.

Helen Bamber Foundation

A human rights charity founded by Helen Bamber. Tel: 020 8058 2020. Website: www.helenbamber.org

* * *

Richard Adams FNIMH, MCPP, MBHMA, MCOM, is an established medical herbalist. He enjoys a family practice in Greenwich, London, that is informed by medical science while rooted in the holistic western tradition. Tel: 0208 691 6938. Website: www.richardadamsherbalist.co.uk

7
Wild Thing, You Make My Heart Sing
Animal Poetry and Ecopsychology

Victoria Field

Psychology concerns itself with how we perceive the world, what brings us joy or pain, how we grow, change and find meaning. Ecopsychology is concerned with integrating the psyche with Nature – seeing one as part of the other, not as two separate entities. Eco comes from *oikos*, the Greek word for household – if we take our household as being the whole planet, we share it with an amazing, in both senses of the word, variety of creatures, human and otherwise. I believe our spiritual health depends on the quality of our relationships in our greater-than-human household. Ecopsychology, with its emphasis on connectedness and unity, works towards the healing of the individual and the planet – one cannot happen without the other.

Poetry has many definitions – its Greek root, *poesis*, simply means a 'thing made' – usually of words and sounds.

To 'make poems' is a natural human impulse. From infancy we experiment with rhyme and repetition and later we may spontaneously shape complex emotions into poetry, especially when we are moved by wonder, love or grief. Reading or making a poem can help us make sense of experiences and connect us more closely to the web of life. It can be profoundly healing, both emotionally and spiritually. In his film about Dartmoor, Satish Kumar (2008) described the landscape as a living poem and we talk of the 'spirit of place'. The words inspiration and spirit are closely related to breath – poems are formed from the breath of life.

Mary Oliver, one of America's best loved poets, writes "I believe everything has a soul". After a difficult childhood, the two blessings of "the natural world, and the world of writing: literature" provided gates through which she says "I vanished from a difficult place". She continues, "the beauty and mystery of the world, out in the fields, or deep inside books – can re-dignify the worststrung heart" (Oliver, 2004, pp.12-13). Her animal poems are reverential, full of the wonder and surprise that comes from closely observing wild creatures. In her poem *The Summer Day* she says "I don't know exactly what a prayer is./ I do know how to pay attention" (Oliver, 1992, p.94). Writing or reading a poem is a way of paying close attention to the world around us and has much in common with prayer. In busy, distracted lives, writing a poem, like making a drawing, can make us focus and find a still centre.

I began drafting this article as I walked a friend's dog on the cliff path in Cornwall on a mild Sunday morning in early January. The world was washed by rain, a necklace of saucer-shaped clouds lay on the horizon, the sea was calm and dotted with pockets of sunlight. Bandit mostly ran ahead, his whole body quivering as he sniffed at tussocks and bits of hedge and rolled in some badger scat, turning frequently to see where I was before suddenly changing direction, attracted by something unseen. He was enjoying a different kind of walk; his world is a tantalising palate of scents which I, with my more primitive nose, can only partly experience. It's probably anthropocentric to talk of him 'enjoying' the walk but that's how it seems. He certainly enhances my walk – making me aware of a world at a different height, the way a single gorse bush can be endlessly absorbing, the curiosity and pleasure aroused by meeting another dog.

Mark Doty and Chase Twichell write movingly of emotions inspired by those animals who as close family members bridge the gap between the domestic and the wild, between consciousness and instinct. In *New Dog*, Doty describes how a man dying of AIDs, who can no longer feed himself, finds strength to lift his hand onto the "rough gilt flanks" of a dog and says how he has "never seen a touch/ so deliberate./ It isn't about grasping ... such attention brought/ to the work" (Doty, 1995, pp.62-3). In *Thinning Shadow of Mimi*, Twichell watches her dying cat, "Soon I'll feel only a draught in her place,/ but that's true of everything I love./ These tears must come from a well/ I didn't know was there" (Twichell, 2006, p.62). Living our daily life closely beside another species can help us experience the world more directly, non-verbally and surprise us with the simplicity of unconditional love.

In many spiritual traditions, reverential interaction

with animals is a way of creating an awareness of the divine (whether conceived of as God, Goddess or Nature herself). In Britain, many churches have windows depicting St Francis preaching to the birds, suggesting "God's care for the whole of … creation, not just people" (Taylor, 2003). In his moving poem, *St Francis and the Sow*, Galway Kinnell (2003) depicts a sow, with her "great broken heart" being reminded of her "loveliness". The poem is outwardly simple. It describes the way all beings can "flower again from within, of self-blessing". In the poem, St Francis tells the sow "in words and in touch/ blessings of the earth". The word blessing is closely related to 'wound' (*blessure* in French) and a love of the world in all its woundedness is a task of ecopsychology. These are ideas that can be conveyed intellectually but the power of the poem comes from its emotional directness, succinctness and specificity. We fully imagine "the long, perfect loveliness of sow" in the description of this particular animal and feel the healing power of the blessings of the Earth.

That morning, the cliff path was busy with blackbirds. They gave no warning cries but every five minutes or so, birds crossed in front of me, fluttering from one blackthorn bush to another. Maybe the mild weather was encouraging them to feed or explore. I walked quietly, thrilled at how closely we could pass each other. In many cultures, birds symbolise the human spirit – we sense joy in their song and see some of our own concerns reflected in their busyness in spring and their attentive parenting. The ability to fly is rich in metaphoric possibilities. Poetry reflects this variousness – Ted Hughes' famous *Hawk Roosting* captures the solitary bird of prey in its magnificence (Hughes,

1995 p.29). A poetry therapist in the US described to me how this poem was helpful in encouraging boys in a detention centre to talk about their experiences by identifying with the bird or its prey. Poetry can open a window or create a safe space for talking about difficult or personal subjects. By using poetry about animals, the natural environment can become part of a therapeutic process for individuals that rebuilds connections with the whole living world.

Western society is suffering an epidemic of depression and anxiety. Writers such as Oliver James and Tom Hodgkinson attribute this to late capitalism, a form of "affluenza". Both a cause and a symptom of this dis-ease is the severing of the links that connect us with those other creatures who share our planet. Poetry is a way of rebuilding those connections – and as an ecopractice "a poem is not only a making of the world, but also a response to the world and a respecting of the earth" (Bate, 2000, p.282). WH Auden claimed "poetry makes nothing happen" – except, that is internally, creating shifts in perspectives that can deepen an ecopsychological perspective on the world. Jonathan Bate describes how poet John Clare was captivated by birds' nests – a structure that human beings are incapable of building. We can though, in poetry, "make a verbal nest by gathering and cherishing odd scraps of language, the words which stand in for the bits and pieces of hay, rotten leaf and feather" (Bate, 2000, p.160).

Ecopoetry is a relatively new term – more than Nature poetry, it emphasises the relationship between humanity and nature. Some animal poems are 'ecopoetry', others may be anthropocentric and yet others act as a metaphor for the poet's feelings. The introduction to Neil Astley's anthology *Earth Shattering* discusses these distinctions. In ecopsychology, all these kinds of poems have a role to play in understanding ourselves in relation to the planet. The imaginative act of reading or writing a poem can illuminate and clarify. To give a few examples, Ted Hughes characterises inspiration as a fox, Denise Levertov writes of grief as a homeless dog and Jane Tozer experiences regret as a woodpecker hammering in a Finnish forest. According to Matthew Fox, the Daoist tradition sees close observation of animals as a spiritual practice (Fox, 2004, pp.164-5). The crane teaches humanity about vigilance and movement, the tiger represents energy and force and can be both noble and a killer. The work of ecopsychology and poetry is to relate these meanings to the individual and simultaneously the individual to the world.

Naturalist Richard Mabey in *Nature Cure*, his memoir of a severe depression and recovery, says that passive appreciation of Nature simply alienated him further. He writes, "What healed me, I think, was almost the exact opposite process, a sense of being taken not out of myself but back in, of nature entering me, firing up the wild bits of my imagination ... those first stumbling imaginative acts ... reconnected me, more than the autumn breeze through the trees" (Mabey 2006, p.224).

This is what poetry can do. We can engage with all animals – from companions who share our literal home, or inhabit our gardens or urban environments – birds, small mammals, insects, invertebrates – to creatures we see infrequently, such as an owl flying over a country lane, a doe and her fawn at dawn, and more distant, animals in wilderness environments, as well as those suffering directly from human action – in zoos or on farms, driven from their habitats or hunted. Active, imaginative engagement can deepen our connection with them, ourselves and each other, helping us to become Thomas Berry's communion of subjects – sharing this wonderful, wounded, blessed Earth.

Reading and writing poetry is a way of co-creating the world and reaffirming ourselves as part of the great web of life. As Denise Levertov writes, the purpose of the web is "to link, not to entrap". She continues "all praise, all praise to the great web" (Levertov, 2002, p.174).

Note
Some of the material in this piece was presented at Naturally, Writing Heals, a conference organised by the Kingfisher Project held at Salisbury Arts Centre in November 2007.

References
Astley, Neil. *Earth Shattering: Ecopoems*, Bloodaxe, 2007.
Bate, Jonathan. *The Song of the Earth*, Picador 2000.
Doty, Mark. *Atlantis: Poems*, Harper Perennial, 1995.
Fox, Matthew. *Creativity: Where the Divine and Human Meet*, Penguin, 2004.
Hodgkinson, Tom. *How to Be Free*, Penguin, 2007.
Hughes, Ted. *New Selected Poems 1957-1994*, Faber & Faber, 1995
James, Oliver. *Affluenza*, Vermillion, 2007.
Kinnell, Galway. *St Francis and the Sow*, in Roger Housden's *Ten Poems to Open Your Heart*, Hodder and Stoughton, 2003.
Kumar, Satish. *Earth Pilgrim – A Year on Dartmoor*, BBC 2 Natural

World. 18th January 2008.
Levertov, Denise. *Selected Poems*, New Directions, 2002.
Mabey, Richard. *Nature Cure*, Pimlico, 2006.
Oliver, Mary. *The Summer Day*, in *New and Selected Poems*, Beacon Press, 1992.
Oliver, Mary. *Wild Geese: Selected Poems*, Bloodaxe Books, 2004.
Saunders, Nicholas. *Animal Spirits*, Macmillan, 1995.
Taylor, Richard. *How to Read a Church*, Random House, 2003.
Twichell, Chase. *Dog Language*, Bloodaxe Books, 2006.

Further Reading

Abbs, Peter. *Earth Songs*, Green Books, 2002.
BBC. *The Nation's Favourite Animal Poems*, BBC, 2001.
Bolton, G, Field, V, and Thompson, K (Eds). *Writing Works: A Handbook of Therapeutic Writing Workshops and Exercises*, Jessica Kingsley, 2006.
Field, Victoria. *Many Waters*, Fal Publications, 2006.
McEwen, Christian, and Statman, Mark. *The Alphabet of the Trees: A Guide to Nature Writing*, Teachers & Writers Collaborative, 2000.

* * *

Victoria Field is a writer and poetry therapist based in Canterbury. Her recent books include a memoir of walking to Santiago: *Baggage: A Book of Leavings* (Francis Boutle, 2016). She is a tutor for the Professional Writing Academy and an International Fellow at Canterbury Christ Church University. See www.thepoetrypractice.co.uk

8
The Paws that Heal

Margaret Lee

Pets are an integral part of many families and I, like many others, grew up with dogs, cats, rabbits and even white mice, which were much appreciated by my siblings but not my mother. As pet owners our animals help us exercise, meet new friends and relax at home – lowering blood pressure and relieving anxieties. They are our friends and confidantes, always happy to see us. If we are sick, disabled, old, lonely we need contact with other kinds of animals as well as humans.

There are a number of voluntary groups who work in this field using their own pets, bringing them into hospitals, care homes, disability centres and even schools, where children with reading problems can read stories to a relaxed animal, forgetting the adult sitting close by.

Pets as Therapy is the largest organisation of its kind in the UK. It is a registered charity, begun in 1983, and has about five thousand dogs and around a hundred cats making regular therapeutic visits.

Therapy Dogs Nationwide, also a registered UK charity,

only began in 2016 and is managed by volunteers. There are many therapy groups using animals both in the UK and in other countries. More information is available on the Internet.

I first read about Pets as Therapy in a magazine article many years ago and thought it was a great idea. However I taught in a primary school and lived in a community and dog owning was not possible. So the idea went on the back burner.

In 2007 I finally re-homed a dog from the RSPCA. Her name was Muffin. After six months I applied for an assessment for her as a therapy pet. During those six months I discovered that I owned a lively, lovable dog but one who had no idea of recall or walking on a lead. She chased bikes and hunted rabbits! In spite of this I decided to give her a chance with the assessment. The day finally came; the venue, a car park near a local wildlife park! The assessor explained she would be watching Muffin's reactions to every movement around us as I walked her on the lead, allowing her to be stroked, ears, tail and feet played with, treats offered and finally a metal tray dropped behind us. I prayed that there were no squirrels, rabbits or bikes in the area to make matters worse. We were about an hour. Muffin was fantastic. She walked, sat, played and totally ignored the noises around her.

We became therapy visitors, volunteering to go to a local care home. Muffin had a yellow jacket and collar with a photo ID. When she wore them she was no longer the busy hunter but a quiet, calm, gentle dog.

The home had five units. Three were residential, one was for nursing and the third was a secure dementia unit. We visited each of them every week, spending time with both residents and staff. Not everyone approved of a dog but slowly over the weeks Monday became 'pat a dog day'! Not exactly a posh title but appropriate. I would take Muffin into each lounge and she would jump on the stool and allow herself to be hugged, patted and sometimes walked in the grounds on a double lead. Sometimes the local church choir would arrive and the lounge would empty, however Muffin took to joining in the singing so after that there was always a following – maybe not for the right reason!

Muffin had the knack of finding the people who were unhappy or having a bad day. Sometimes members of staff called me in to see certain residents. One could be quite violent and would hit out, throwing objects at both staff and residents. Muffin would walk into the room, snuggling up with head and front paws resting gently on her knees. Within minutes the woman would be calm and hugging Muffin. Another, whose name was Jo, and who was suffering from depression, would not get out of bed. Muffin would stand at her door and bark to get her attention then would walk to the lounge and wait. Sure enough, before we left the building Jo would be helped into the lounge by a carer and Muffin would make a fuss of her.

There is a waiting list for Therapy Pets and I was asked if I would take Muffin to another home to see how the residents there would react. We visited each area and a few wanted to talk and stroke Muffin. On the way out one of the carers called me and said there was a woman in the room with dementia; she had not spoken or responded to anything for at least the last year, however they did know that she used to own a dog. I went in the room and there were several carers around saying to the woman, "Look here's a dog", and "give me your hand and stroke the dog" but there was no response, just an emptiness in her eyes. Muffin took things in hand. She jumped on the empty chair next to the woman and put a paw on her arm. Then she climbed onto the arm of the chair and gave her a gentle lick to her cheek. The woman's eyes came to life, her hands stretched out and pulled Muffin's ears saying, "dog a dog". Muffin stayed still whilst she had her tail, ears and feet pulled, her fur ruffled and even her eyes poked. Then the woman's eyes again went empty. Muffin gently licked her face climbed off the chair and walked away. There were tears in that room. Just for a few minutes something akin to a miracle had happened.

Most days were not exceptional they were just ordinary visits to people who loved Muffin and were loved by her. We continued visiting the same care home for six years, meeting new residents and saying goodbye to others. Muffin greeted and amused them all, and because of her the home allowed the families to bring in pets to help with recovery and to make it more homely. Muffin would greet any other animal in the lounge before visiting her friends.

Muffin's visits ended when she was diagnosed with lymphoma three years ago and we retired from official therapy work because of treatment and possible infections both to Muffin and to the elderly residents.

We both miss our Monday visits. Muffin still engages in her favourite pastimes of hunting and cycle chasing, and on her walks she is known and greeted by everyone, her zest for life and mischief putting a smile on the saddest face.

Relevant Websites
petsastherapy.org
therapydogsnationwide.org

*   *   *

Margaret Lee is a Sister of Notre Dame de Namur living in Liverpool. She began teaching in primary education in the north of England and London and later working with the Travelling People. Returning to Britain, after spending some time in Peru, she attended Goldsmith's College in London qualifying as an art psychotherapist. She returned to Liverpool where she worked as an art therapist in a school for children with autism and provided personal therapy for university students training as art and music therapists.

PART THREE
IMPLEMENTING GREEN WISDOM

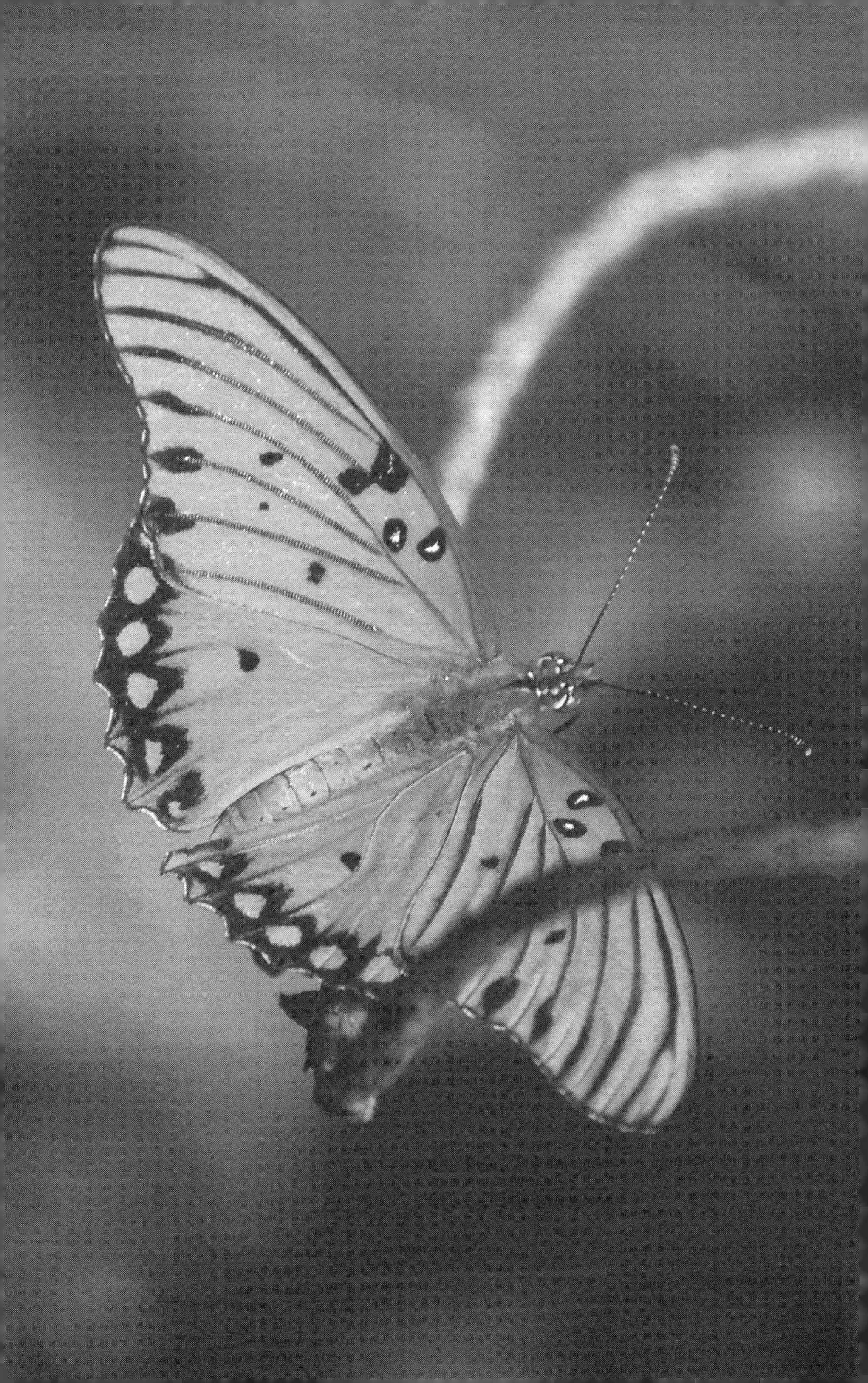

9
Project Green Hands

Katie Hill

We're sitting on a baked clay floor, drinking fresh juice made from a fruit I can't identify (and still couldn't place even after I'd heard its name). We're in Sathyamangalam, Tamil Nadu, India, visiting a farmer who recently decided to revert to the organic farming methods that sustained India's farmers for thousands of years – and that were largely rejected at the dawn of the Green Revolution.

His father was one of many seduced by hybrid seeds, chemical fertilisers, artificial pesticides and monocrop farming. The land around us had, until recently, been crammed with cash crops – sugar cane, banana plants and coconut palms – that yielded maximum return for minimal labour. One man with a fertiliser gun could do the work of 15-20 weed-pickers. He'd built the business up with a comfortable retirement in mind – and felt he was now watching it crumble before his eyes as his son pursued a hopeless dream of 'going natural'.

The monsoon – which is also known as the real finance minister of India – had bypassed Sathyamangalam for three consecutive years, leaving the land thirsty and the rivers dry. Without sufficient water the land hadn't been able to make much of a transition to an operational organic farm and the family was forced to live on savings – but it was still several steps ahead of neighbours who persisted with monocrop systems. Those who hadn't yet felt the full, devastating force of a third year with no rain would do so the following year – and then they'd need to decide whether to strip their barren land bare or switch to a more sustainable alternative.

The decision to rip out lucrative cash crops and adopt an alien system of farming was a brave one that was rewarded with disgust from his father and rejection from his community. It was a huge risk taken at a climactically uncertain time – so why do it?

The family was supported by a grassroots ecological initiative established by Isha Foundation, which is based out of a local ashram in the Velliangiri foothills near Coimbatore. The overall goal of 'Project Green Hands' is to increase Tamil Nadu's green cover to the required 33% by planting 114 million trees.

Encouraging the switch to organic farming is one of the ways in which Project Green Hands is increasing the state's green cover. Many farmers assume that planting trees could inhibit the growth of crops, so volunteers with the project conduct awareness camps to educate farmers and inspire them to plant saplings alongside their crops.

As a next step, farmers who decide to go organic are sold trees of ecological and economic benefit as an insurance policy; if their crops fail during the transition to chemical-free farming, the trees can be cut down and sold as a last resort. In the meantime, fruit from the trees and black peppercorns from vines that grow up the trunks can be harvested and sold.

The additional income from the trees and secondary crops can offset the farmer's loss of income from the reduction in the main crop. The farm will then become sustainable and profitable within seven years.

Volunteers with Project Green Hands want farmers to see the trees as an investment, so the saplings aren't given away for free. Instead, farmers pay the price of a cup of chai – something everyone can afford – and see each tree as having a value of its own. The fact that at least one crop can be harvested from each of the trees also dissuades farmers from cutting the trees down prematurely for sale as timber.

As well as acting as an insurance policy, the trees bring additional benefits to the land. Planting trees on farmland reduces soil erosion, increases soil fertility, water retention capacity and total available nutrients, which results in a larger yield of the primary crop.

Previously the only reason farmers planted trees on their land was to protect the valuable banana plants against their greatest threat, the wind – but farmers involved with the project are now starting to see trees as an asset in their own right.

When mixed with crops trees create individual microclimates that protect plants from harsh, direct sunlight. The shade creates a forest environment which will become increasingly valuable as global temperatures continue to rise. The trees also attract birds to the land, which is a huge bonus.

There are 14 species of pest that attack the crops but 48 species of bird that attack these pests, so bumping up the number of birds visiting the land will help the farm to thrive naturally.

Still, not everyone is sure about the supremacy of organic farming; of the 10 local farmers who agreed to join the Trees for Life programme, six dropped out in the first eight months because they weren't seeing results of their transition to organic farming quickly enough.

It takes faith and trust to adopt a different course, and many of the farmers who have continued along their organic path have done so because of their trust in Sadhguru, the founder of Isha Foundation and instigator of Project Green Hands.

A mystic, yogi and 'visionary humanitarian', Sadhguru has dedicated the last three decades of his life to revitalising the ancient spiritual sciences that formed the fabric of India's cultural ethos. Based out of an ashram in Tamil Nadu, the Isha Foundation doesn't promote any particular ideology, religion or race; instead it transmits inner sciences 'of universal appeal' and addresses the practical, local issues around globalisation and climate change.

Sadhguru has often said that "society is overripe for a spiritual process"; while technological advances have brought us luxuries and comforts, he believes most human beings still remain "in search of wholeness". As a result, his mission is to offer "one drop of spirituality" to every human being, so that we can all experience the deepest core of life within. He does this by mixing "the right cocktail" of kriya (energy), bhakti (devotion), gnana (knowledge) and karma (action) for each individual, as he believes we're all a unique combination of these four paths of yoga.

Project Green Hands is Sadhguru's response to the deforestation and environmental degradation in the state of Tamil Nadu. He saw that nurturing two saplings over the next 10 years was a task that even the poorest of the poor could do, and that the rich and the resourceful had the ability to do much more.

Sadhguru engineered Project Green Hands so that every single person's simple involvement and personal action could make something truly beautiful, wonderful and timely happen – without placing any additional financial burden on the state.

With the help of 1.5 million volunteers, the project has planted over 19.9 million saplings in Tamil Nadu and Pondicherry. In 2006, over 250,000 volunteers planted 852,587 saplings in just three days, earning the project a place in the *Guinness Book of World Records*. The Indian government has recognised Project Green Hands' positive ecological impact and awarded it the Indira Gandhi Paryavaran Puraskar – India's highest environmental award.

Many of the volunteers are derived from local schools, under a separate 'Green School' initiative that's also run by Isha Foundation. The aim of this initiative is to create a 'green consciousness' and a sense of pride in environmental conservation among the next generation.

In a district, between 200 and 300 schools are chosen to be part of the Green School Movement, subject to the approval of the district Chief Educational Officer (CEO). Project Green Hands offers seeds, covers for the saplings,

Teachers from schools taking part in the Green School initiative.

workshops and technical guidance for sapling production, and then teaches students how to start a nursery in their own school. Each school is then given enough seeds and covers to raise 2,000 saplings, which are meant to be planted in the school premises or distributed to other schools in the district.

The Green School movement was first launched as a pilot project of nearly 300 schools in Erode district. Each school had a target to produce and plant 2,000 saplings in the year 2011, meaning the district's schoolchildren contributed to the planting of almost 600,000 saplings. On the back of this success, the Education Department of Coimbatore adopted the programme in its district – and 19,440 students from over 200 schools participated and were directly involved in producing and nurturing 285,040 saplings as a result.

The school children help to produce and plant saplings and are rewarded for their work and participation. Rather than tying conservation to the curriculum, it's delivered as an outdoor experience that's fun, engaging and deeply imprinted in each child's mind.

We went to visit a school that had opted in to the Green School programme and the children were having the time of their lives. Sitting in long lines on the ground under a green tarpaulin, they chatted and giggled as they stuffed small bags with soil.

These bags would house the saplings that would eventually transform into trees, and which would bear fruit that could generate a life-saving income for local farmers. These trees would also eventually help improve the health of the land on which the children's food – and perhaps the children's children's food – would grow, and help organic agriculture return to India.

* * *

Katie Hill writes on consumer affairs and all things green. She is passionate about the environment, Hindu philosophy and finding new ways for younger generations to connect with Nature.

10
Elephant Protection
An Interview with Susan Canney

Ian Mowll

How did you get involved in elephant protection?

I trained in natural sciences and specialised in zoology. Following a doctorate studying human impact on a Tanzanian National Park, it seemed that the work that came my way was about trying to find ways to accommodate elephants in a world that is increasingly dominated by humans. As a result I have been working on elephant projects since 2000 in Asia and Africa, and in Mali since 2003.

I think the worldwide acceleration in habitat destruction associated with globalisation and rising populations has meant the encroachment of human populations into elephant habitat. While other species 'quietly disappear' when this happens, elephants still try to find the food and resources they need. This has led to increasing human elephant conflict as elephants eat the crops that have taken the place of their forest homes.

Although elephant protection is the initial focus, dealing with the underlying cause requires engaging with the wider context and a complex nexus of environment, people, politics and society.

What are the problems that elephants face?
Elephants face two major problems. The first, described above, involves humans encroaching into their habitat and clearing it for agriculture, commercial plantations and infrastructure development.

The second is that elephants are being killed for their ivory tusks. Before firearms were invented it was thought there were around 10 million elephants in Africa. Their numbers were halved in the 1970s and 1980s, prompting a 1989 international ban on the trade of ivory by the Convention on International Trade in Endangered Species (CITES). As a result elephant numbers began to recover in the 1990s in many areas, opening the door for a partial lifting of the ban for the elephant populations in Botswana, Namibia, Zimbabwe and South Africa, and one-off sales of ivory to Japan in 2002 and to China and Japan in 2008.

Some argued that this would limit poaching by flooding the market, causing prices to crash and making poaching less profitable. Others warned that it would unleash explosive demand, and a rise in the price of ivory that would trigger a surge in the poaching of illegal ivory that could be 'laundered' by the legal markets of China. The latter camp was correct, but underestimated the impact because the billion-dollar industry has attracted organised criminal networks – the same people who traffic drugs, people and arms – who feed the increased demand in Asia as a result of a rise in disposable wealth, with about 70% of illegal ivory ultimately destined for China. In addition it appears that speculators are stockpiling ivory (and rhino horn) assuming the price will increase as elephants (and rhinos) disappear.

The result is that there are now approximately 350,000 African elephants left and they are being lost at a rate of around 27,000 per year.

These two problems are interlinked where poor, marginalised people seek land and encroach into elephant habitat, or bear the impacts of elephants displaced by large-scale clearance for plantations or mono-cultures, or live adjacent to protected areas from which they are excluded to benefit tourists and others more wealthy and powerful than they are. Young men with no employment or prospects are vulnerable to recruitment by trafficking networks that want ivory.

How do elephants help us, other animals and the environment in general?

Elephants help in many different ways and at different levels. Most obviously, they regenerate forests by spreading the seeds of trees excreted in dung, so the seeds start their life in their own little 'grow bag' of compost. Germination and seedling survival are much higher for seeds given such a good start in life. An adult elephant produces about one tonne of manure every week and in the process fertilises the soils by spreading nutrients across the landscape.

Elephants disperse more seeds of more tree species than any other animal – and further. Tree species with large seeds need big animals to disperse them, and some forest tree species have seeds that actually require passage through an elephant's gut to be able to germinate.

In addition, botanists have reported that tree species with large seeds tend to store more carbon per unit volume of wood, meaning forests with elephants and other large animals are better carbon sinks.

Elephants open up woodland thickets, releasing nutrients into the ecosystem and providing food and shelter for other animals. For example a multitude of lizards rely on the cover provided by the debris created by elephants to escape the piercing talons of a hungry raptor.

In Mali, local people speak of elephants knocking down otherwise inaccessible fruits and seeds from high branches that are gathered by the women for food and sometimes sale. Fruits and leaves are also eaten by livestock that gather around their feet, while dung is valued for helping conjunctivitis, a widespread problem in these environments.

Elephants dig for water in dry river beds and, once the water hole has been created, other animals can access the water, helping the whole ecosystem.

When we asked local people in Mali what they thought about elephants, the predominant view was that elephants are an indicator of a healthy and diverse ecosystem that is more productive and resilient to environmental change. The ecosystem forms the basis of their livelihoods and a part of their identity: if the ecosystem thrives, they thrive.

Most said they feel a sense of awe when they witness elephants' social interactions and the wide range of emotions they express. They also feel that every species has a right to exist and that it contributes something unique to the ecosystem. This notion was described to me as being encapsulated in the word *baraka*, or blessing. Each species has its own *baraka*, and if a species is lost, the ecosystem is irretrievably diminished and poorer in its ability to sustain life.

Can you tell us about elephant behaviour?
Local people have numerous anecdotes about elephants. In Mali they talk about their joy when groups reunite, the closeness of their family groups and their apparent care for each other – particularly for their young.

They have reported seeing elephants covering their dead with soil and branches and several individuals standing vigil for a number of days. Such 'death rituals' have been widely reported and all seem to include a calm descending over the elephants as they gently explore the bones. Sometimes they pick them up and turn them over. During this process they are definitely in a different state from their usual way of being and their temporal gland streams, a sure sign of emotion. It is not known why they do this. Maybe their body-mind complex needs to process the emotions or maybe, like humans, it's part of their social bonding.

In Indonesia local people say that elephants need the primary forests not so much for food but for peace to have their babies. They described how elephant 'midwives' stand in a circle around an elephant who was giving birth protecting and stroking the pregnant mother, swaying and making sounds with her. They assist the newborn's release from the amniotic sac, then help it stand up and take its first steps.

In Mali they speak of their cleverness: in one incident elephants constructed a causeway of wood and branches to help rescue another elephant stuck in mud. They also spoke of their tolerance and how they rarely hurt humans, despite much provocation and many opportunities to do so. One anecdote was when an elephant was lying down next to a small water hole and some children climbed on to the elephant to play on its back. There was no response from the elephant until they lit a fire, at which point the elephant sucked up some water and squirted it onto its back, shook off the children, got up and walked away!

In India the story was that in the past when elephants were used for logging, bells were hung around their necks so that the workers could tell when they were raiding crops at night, however the elephants scooped up mud and stuck it inside the bells so they could not be heard during their night-time adventures.

How is the sacred important in your work?

The role of the sacred is to recognise the whole and to 'draw the line', to establish limits that bring people together as equal. All the qualities of elephants discussed above are much greater when taken together, something that is recognised in the concept of *baraka*.

I am sometimes asked, "Why does your work in resource management need the elephants? Surely you can achieve all those things without invoking the need to protect elephants". However, if 'sacred' is used to denote something that is so important that it is unquestioningly respected by all, the elephants provide a vital unifying element and focus that applies to everyone – whether one is a powerful chief, a peasant, rich, poor, from a village or a distant town. Without this the process is vulnerable to derailment by multiple agendas as there are always elements of society trying to get more than their fair share – by whatever means!

What is your contribution to elephant protection?
We deal with a huge area, almost the size of Switzerland. After spending three years understanding the elephant migration I realised that the only way the elephants would survive was if the day-to-day activities of the 265,000+ people who live in this area were supportive of elephant conservation. And so we spent the next three years discussing our results with local people, asking them what they thought, how they experienced elephants in their lives and what they thought could be done about conflicts. At the same time we used this engagement to build a common vision throughout Mali that these elephants must be protected.

The area was suffering from over-use and degradation, both from the influx of people seeking land and from the impact of globalisation on the urban areas. Commercial charcoal and firewood operations plundered the local woodlands, and a study revealed that 96% of the cattle using a key lake belonged to wealthy individuals living in distant towns who amassed huge herds of cattle as signs of prestige.

A key problem was that each different ethnicity in the area had its own system of resource management but would not obey the others', which resulted in a 'free-for-all' that led to habitat destruction and degradation. This diminished local subsistence livelihoods and created competition between clans and ethnicities – and between humans and elephants.

So we brought the different clans and ethnicities of a community together to discuss the problem until they arrived at a shared understanding. Then they have to work out solutions. Invariably this means electing a representative management committee of elders who determine the rules of resource use, including the areas to protect as important elephant habitat. Teams of young men ('eco-guardians') patrol to detect infringements of the rules and conduct resource protection activities such as building fire-breaks and planting trees.

Studies have shown that livestock from communities protecting their water, pasture and forests are worth 50% more than those from communities that don't have functioning resource management systems. At the same time, those managing their pasture are able to sell hay and charge outsiders for access to water and pasture. As they say, 'We benefit twice: we have more pasture for ourselves and we raise money from others' – and in doing so, they control the destructive impact of the 'prestige herds'.

This process of collective resource management promotes reconciliation and builds solidarity to resist the current insecurity. It also prevents the radicalisation of the youth by providing an alternative to taking up arms. Most prefer this option because, although they do not reap the financial rewards offered by the jihadist groups, they have an occupation that carries local prestige within the community and that's less risky. During the conflict of 2012–13 not one of the 520 eco-guardians joined the jihadist groups, despite being offered $30–$50 a day to do so.

* * *

Susan Canney is the director of the Mali Elephant Project (see www.wild.org/mali-elephants), a conservation adviser to WILD Foundation, a research associate of the Department of Zoology at the University of Oxford, and a trustee of Tusk Trust. She co-authored *Conservation* for Cambridge University Press, which takes a global perspective for bringing conservation to the heart of sustainability and environmental policy.

11
Spirituality & Veganism

Piers Warren

Veganism (as defined by The Vegan Society) is a way of living which seeks to exclude, as far as it is possible and practicable, all forms of exploitation of, and cruelty to, animals for food, clothing or any other purpose.

But is there any connection between veganism and spirituality? Amongst the aims of GreenSpirit, you will see that GreenSpirit challenges us to "replace the anthropocentric worldview with an ecocentric one" and to "walk ever more lightly on the Earth". These challenges in particular tie in very clearly with vegan ideals.

To explore the advantages of veganism let me give you a run through of my own journey. As a young child I was drawn to animals and being outside in Nature. My earliest memories include the joy of finding slow worms under logs and building little ponds for tadpoles. From around the age of seven, I began growing my own veg (just radishes and lettuce to start with), which has grown into a passion that will stay with me my whole life.

Early on I also realised there was a lot of cruelty and exploitation in the world – elephants being massacred for their ivory, for example – and this realisation led to my later work in conservation. However, like most people in the UK, I was brought up eating meat and drinking milk and didn't really make the connection between this and cruelty; it was just the way things were. Plus of course we were victims of marketing hype telling us how healthy milk was, despite the incongruity that in the wild no other animal drinks another species' milk, and none drink milk beyond weaning.

As my interest in animal welfare grew I became a vegetarian as a young adult, and this decision was reinforced by a period living just down the lane from a large modern abattoir (the day-long screaming from the pigs stays with me to this day). I was also interested in self-sufficiency, yet my attempts at running a smallholding met the dilemmas of what to do with surplus male chicks, and the distress of removing young goat kids from their mother so that she could be milked for our own consumption.

The idea that veganism was the way to go to relieve my troubled conscience came to me, but it was years until I made the effort to embrace it fully. Like many vegetarians I struggled with doing without milk, cheese and eggs and managed to keep putting it to the back of my mind despite knowing that I would take the plunge one day.

Four things pushed me closer to the inevitable. Firstly, through organisations like VIVA! (see resources at the end of this article), I learnt more about the cruelty involved in the dairy and egg industries: young calves torn away from their mothers at birth to be shot or sent to veal crates overseas; millions of day-old male chicks (useless for egg production) tossed live into a grinder, not to mention the awful conditions most laying birds are kept in, free-range or not, and so on. It is said that there is more cruelty in a glass of milk than a pound of steak. The animals we eat, from cattle to chickens to fish, are sentient beings with complex relationships with each other. Above all they want to avoid pain and not die. Research shows that even lobsters and crabs feel pain – being out of water for many hours before being boiled alive is not a good way to go.

Secondly, I learnt more about the personal health benefits of a cruelty-free diet. Vegans are less likely to suffer from all the major diseases: cancer, heart problems, diabetes, obesity etc. Increasingly the major health and dietetic organisations worldwide are encouraging people to eat less meat and more fruit and veg. This was driven home by the tragedy of losing my sister (who ate a lot of meat and dairy) who, despite being fit and having never smoked, died quickly of liver cancer in her fifties.

Thirdly, it became clear that the meat and dairy industries were major contributors to climate change (more than all the world's transport systems put together). With my work in conservation, my horror at the dire projections as CO_2 emissions continue to increase and my own desire to reduce my carbon footprint, it seemed hypocritical to put off turning vegan myself. It may feel easier to switch to a green energy supplier or use public transport more, but the greatest thing you can personally do to reduce climate change is to become vegan. The effects of the meat and dairy industries on the climate, and why they are covered up, are explored in the excellent film *Cowspiracy* (see resources). There are many other ecological disasters associated with the drive for animal protein: for example, current projections are that by 2050 there will be no viable stocks of fish left in the oceans – worldwide.

And finally, as my own explorations into spirituality developed I kept coming back to the three words 'respect for life'. I've never been anthropocentric, have never considered man above all other animals – we've just evolved differently. I've always loved all animals, been fascinated by them and the wonder of evolution, found great peace in Nature, and been awe-inspired by the beauty of wild places and creatures. I could not be a part of the wheel of destruction and cruelty purely through a liking for the taste of meat or cheese or milk. We are all connected. How can we feel spiritually at peace when we are causing so much death and cruelty every day (more than a billion animals are slaughtered for food every year in the UK alone)? There is nothing humane or ethical about slaughterhouses, no matter how modern they are. If you're not sure what goes on then I urge you to watch the documentary *Earthlings* (see resources). It's a harrowing experience, but then if just watching a film is traumatising, imagine what the reality is like. Not caring about the lives of sentient beings does not fit in with my idea of spirituality at all. There is nothing less valuable about the lives of pigs (which are more intelligent than dogs) than the pets we love and care for. I want to continue to explore and embrace compassion, empathy and reverence for all living beings.

It's been interesting to meet other vegans who had never previously thought of spiritual aspects of their life, but since becoming vegan have explored and embraced spirituality, taken up other activities such as meditation and yoga and gained deeper personal peace.

Respect for life extends to other humans too, of course. A billion people worldwide do not have enough to eat, yet the amount of grain fed to cattle to provide the rich west with burgers could alleviate all hunger in the world. The plant food needed to produce just one pound of meat could feed ten people for an entire day. It is unjust in the extreme.

There are already millions of vegans in the world, living healthy, cruelty-free lives, and more people are joining them all the time as the horrors of the meat and dairy industries are more exposed. It's easier than ever to eat out as a vegan, and more alternatives (such as plant-based milks and cheeses) make it easy to cook at home without feeling like you're missing out on anything. Veganism has boosted my enjoyment of food and cooking, and with the right variety of plant-based wholefoods it's easy to get enough of the right nutrition, protein, vitamins and minerals in a healthier form than you would get from animal products. Increasingly top athletes are turning to a vegan diet as its benefits for health and fitness are discovered.

Our digestive systems and metabolism have evolved to thrive on plant-based diets as increasing amounts of scientific research prove – such as *The China Study* (see resources). The reason people eat so much meat and dairy worldwide is simply because they like the taste – a shallow reason to fund cruelty and climate change at the expense of your own health.

The more I've learnt about veganism, and the longer I've practised it, the happier I've been with the decision to exclude cruelty to animals, as far as possible, from my life, reduce my carbon footprint and improve my health. Like many other vegans I have spoken to I only wish I'd started many years ago, and I know I will never turn back.

Here are Some Resources I've Found Really Useful and Supportive

Organisations:
The Vegan Society (www.vegansociety.com).

VIVA! (www.viva.org.uk) is very active in campaigning against cruelty, plus excellent nutritional advice.

Magazine:
Vegan Life (veganlifemag.com) has lots of interesting articles and news items about vegan topics plus yummy recipes.

Books:
World Peace Diet by Dr Will Tuttle (www.worldpeacediet.com) is a bestselling, in-depth study of our food and culture with a spiritual thread throughout.

The China Study by Dr T Colin Campbell details the connection between nutrition and heart disease, diabetes and cancer. The report also examines the source of nutritional confusion produced by powerful lobbies, government entities and opportunistic scientists.

Films:

Earthlings (www.nationearth.com/earthlings) is a documentary about humankind's total dependence on animals for economic purposes.

Cowspiracy (www.cowspiracy.com) is a groundbreaking feature-length environmental documentary following filmmaker Kip Andersen as he uncovers the most destructive industry facing the planet today – and investigates why the world's leading environmental organisations are too afraid to talk about it.

Editors' Note

If you are a member of GreenSpirit and would like to discuss veganism with other members, then please share your thoughts on the GreenSpirit Members' Facebook page: www.facebook.com/groups/greenspiritmembers

* * *

Piers Warren is a conservationist and the Principal of Wildeye (the International school of Wildlife Film-making). Website: www.wildeye.co.uk. Email: piers@wildeye.co.uk

He is the author of numerous books including *The Vegan Cook and Gardener: Growing, Storing and Cooking Delicious Healthy Food all Year Round* (coauthored with Ella Bee Glendining), and *Conservation Film-making: How to Make Films that Make a Difference*: www.wildeye.co.uk/conservation-film-making-book

12
Down to Earth
An Eco-Friendly Burial

Jean Francis

An entire life could be spent collecting and recycling milk bottle tops. Yet this good deed can be undone instantly by making a thoughtless funeral choice, simply because we haven't investigated the possible environmental impact our funeral may have on our planet.

Although death is a taboo subject, it will happen to us all. I sincerely recommend that we pre-plan our funeral or that of a loved one, allowing time to investigate the many options available. Otherwise, when someone dies a call is made to a funeral director who takes over and presents an often unaffordable bill at the end. The death of someone close to us is an enormous shock but life must continue. Taking responsibility and being aware of our choices means that contrary to belief, funerals do not have to cost the Earth, and the way we choose to depart can make a huge difference to our well-being and that of our planet.

Funerals Do Not Have to Cost a Fortune

There are many ways in which families can take part in the care of a loved one and arrange the funeral themselves, with or without the support of a funeral director. Awareness of the many options available and a bit of forward planning will mean that you are less likely to end up with an impersonal, costly, production-line funeral.

It is also possible to carry out a funeral without using a funeral director. Many independent companies are open to supporting families who wish to be involved themselves, to whatever degree.

Some Points to Consider

A green burial offers the opportunity to plant a tree in memory of a loved one instead of a headstone. Such places become a haven for wildlife and a place of natural beauty for future generations to enjoy, kept safe from developers. To locate a natural burial ground in your area see: www.naturaldeath.org.uk

Cremation has become more popular in recent years. Should you consider being cremated, do be aware that, in spite of strict government legislation, many carcinogenic pollutants in the atmosphere come from crematoria. Bear in mind also the enormous amount of energy required to fuel the cremators.

A Few Green Guidelines for Both Burial and Cremation

• Embalming fluids are toxic and should be avoided wherever possible

- Choose a biodegradable coffin made from natural materials – there are many choices available

- Ensure that the deceased is dressed in natural fabrics

- Choose flowers from the garden or another local area instead of imported or hot-house blooms

- Be aware of carbon footprints when arranging transport

There are many decisions and choices to be made; it is my passion to offer people guidance gained from many years of research and my deep desire to ease people through this process.

Final Wishes Workshop

Freddie was one of 10 people who signed up for my Workshop. Delegates worked steadily through the questionnaire, discussing the options around planning their funerals from beginning to end. Would they choose burial, cremation, medical donation, direct cremation, woodland burial? The consequence of each choice was discussed. Freddie lit up and became especially intrigued when he learned that it is possible to be buried in your own back garden or on private land. We discussed the few legalities involved and there was no stopping him!

By the end of the day delegates were in possession of a personalised folder. This contained their Last Wishes and also many useful hand-outs that would support their next of kin at the time of death. The day ended on a high with much banter and laughter. My own funeral plans change like the weather; I expect theirs will too as, with awareness, new and different ideas come to mind.

Freddie valued this initial stage and we met privately to continue the process. I am a OneSpirit minister, who specialises in creating heart-felt and meaningful funerals. Together, we designed a ceremony that gave Freddy comfort knowing that when he "Pops his clogs", using his words, his nearest and dearest would have little to do. At my suggestion, he left a few decisions for them to make, feeling comforted that he had taken steps to ease any potential strain or trauma.

The Ceremony We Created Together Reflected Freddie's Beliefs, Passions and Philosophies
Freddie followed no particular faith; his roots were firmly in Nature and the beauty of the natural world. He had a deep fascination for Native American culture and was enchanted by magic. He worshiped the goddess, although only a few of his friends were aware of this fact. We therefore honoured his feminine side by subtle references to the moon.

Three Years Had Passed
On the day of Freddie's funeral, as he'd imagined, we gathered beneath an old oak tree to await his arrival. He had chosen a willow casket, decorated with a tangle of contorted willow, blackberry brambles and wild flowers. Freddie was carried to his final resting place by six good friends.

Wearing green wellies beneath my long purple skirt and carrying a lantern containing a burning candle, I led the procession through a wooded area to the graveside. Freddie had chosen this place because of its spectacular views across rolling countryside, where he had spent many happy hours roaming as a boy. His casket was placed gently on supports over the grave as family and friends gathered.

In Freddie's chosen words, everyone was welcomed. We acknowledged that we were going to say farewell to Fredrick Andrew Bates, known to all as Freddie; to mourn his passing but more importantly to celebrate his life. Having explained the significance of the ceremony, I suggested that anyone with differing beliefs should say their goodbyes in a way that would bring them peace and comfort.

Having introduced myself, I explained how Freddie and I had co-created this occasion and his concern over not wanting to burden others with having to make decisions on his behalf. Besides, he had taken responsibility for his life, so why not his death?

In Native American tradition, a circle was cast using cornmeal; creating a sacred space around the grave. As requested, people had brought treasures from Nature: pebbles, leaves, cones, berries, flowers and much more, which they added to the circle.

Facing each of the four directions in turn, we invoked the elements, respectfully requesting that they join us: the element of earth from the North, air from the East, fire from the South and water from the West, without which there would be no life on Earth.

Invocation
*Our Father, the Sky, hear us
and make us strong.
Our Mother, the Earth, hear us
and give us support.
Spirit of the East,
send us your Wisdom.
Spirit of the South,
may we tread your path.
Spirit of the West,
may we always be ready
for the long journey.
Spirit of the North, purify us
with your cleansing winds.*
– OF SIOUX ORIGIN

I spoke about Freddie's interest in Native American culture and several experiences that had touched him deeply.

Freddie's daughter read the Native American Ten Commandments, which personified the way in which Freddie had lived his life:

*Treat the Earth and all that dwell thereon with respect.
Remain close to the Great Spirit, in all that you do.
Show great respect for your fellow beings.
(Especially respect yourself.)
Work together for the benefit of all Mankind.
Give assistance and kindness wherever needed.
Do what you know to be right.*

(But be careful not to fall into self-righteousness.)
Look after the well-being of mind and body.
Dedicate a share of your efforts to the greater good.
Be truthful and honest at all times.
(Especially be truthful and honest with yourself.)
Take full responsibility for your actions.

A pause for reflection offered a time of silence as everyone said goodbye to Freddie in their own way; a silence broken only by distant birdsong and the buzz of a bumble bee.

Harry, Freddie's younger brother, spoke with humour about their childhood and some of the crazy pranks they got up to as lads.

I read the following words from a dog-eared book found beside Freddie's chair:

Oh, Great Spirit, whose voice I hear in the winds and whose breath gives life to all the world, hear me. I am small and weak. I need your strength and wisdom. Let me walk in beauty and make my eyes ever behold the red and purple sunset. Make my hands respect the things you have made and my ears sharp to hear your voice. Make me wise so that I may understand the things you have taught my people. Let me learn the lessons you have hidden in every leaf and rock.

I seek strength, not to be superior to my brother, but to fight my greatest enemy – myself. Make me always ready to come to you with clean hands and straight eyes, so now my life has faded, as the fading sunset, my spirit will come to you without shame.

– CHIEF YELLOW LARK, LAKOTA, 1887

As a country lad, Freddie had a deep knowing that birth, life, death and rebirth are all part of the wheel of Nature. This we honoured, asking for his safe transition into spirit as we laid his human remains to rest into the elements from which he came.

We committed Fredrick Andrew Bates to a retreat of peacefulness. As the coffin was lowered into the grave, together we said the following words:

Freddie, with beauty before you, we let you go,
With beauty behind you, we let you go,
With beauty above you, we let you go,
With beauty below you, we let you go,
With beauty around you, we let you go.

How perfectly Mother Nature has prepared herself to receive you; overlooked by Father Sky, the sunshine by day and, at night, by Grandmother Moon with a canopy of stars overhead. We commit you to the oneness of Nature whence you came, to reconnect with the flow of all that is natural.

Freddie, we place you gently into the embrace of Mother Earth to hold and nurture you into new life as you re-connect with your ancestors. Behold the harmony of the Universe.

We tossed the treasures from Nature into the grave followed by a handful of earth as final farewells were said.

Freddie's passion for magic had not been forgotten. We turned to the four directions, acknowledging their elements; earth, air, fire and water, the sources of energy on which magicians have always called. We gave thanks and honoured their presence.

Closing Blessing
Deep peace of the flowing water to you
Deep peace of the quiet Earth to you
Deep peace of the shining stars to you
Deep peace of the magic moon to you.

Blessed be.

* * *

Everyone met at Freddie's 'local', where fond memories were shared amongst tears of joy and sadness. I felt I'd known this amazing man all my life – we had shared so much during the time spent planning his funeral. Knowing that his wishes had been carried out, exactly as he had requested, was of great comfort to all those who knew him.

Freddie's legacy and final act of kindness was to give back to the precious environment that sustains us all.

* * *

You too can have a unique send-off that reflects your passions, lifestyle and philosophies.

Last Wishes Workshops
www.circleoflifecelebrations.co.uk/last-wishes-workshop/

On-line Funeral Planning
www.circleoflifecelebrations.co.uk/my-services/

* * *

Jean Francis is a funeral arranger and OneSpirit minister. Jean's inspiration comes from Mother Nature and the beauty that surrounds us – equally honouring people of any faith or none. She works with people to create heartfelt and meaningful ceremonies that celebrate all life events, from birth through to funerals.

Jean is author of four books and winner of a major national award: the 'Most Significant Contribution to the understanding of death' for her work on preneed funeral planning, awarded at the Good Funerals Ceremony in Bournemouth 2013.

13
Eco-Restaurant in the Amazon Jungle
An Interview with Nicola Peel

Ian Mowll

How did you start working in this area?

One day, I was down at the beach by a nearby river and I found a spring. Somebody had put stones around it, cleaned it up and made the spring look beautiful. This same person had also made an ecological trail with signs saying such things as "Please collect your rubbish", "Care for the environment" and "Look after the animals".

It's quite unusual to find somebody who cares about Nature like this in Ecuador and so I carried on along the river. I came out into a little village and then I saw the same signs outside a house so I knew it must be the same person. I knocked on the door and there I met Don Walter. I said it was fantastic that he was looking after the spring and cleaning up. He was very happy with my encouragement. But then he looked at me with a sad face and said the problem is that every day he goes down and collects the rubbish and he does not know what to do with it all. He had bags and bags of rubbish. I told him about the bottles and bricks projects in which I am involved. We stuff old plastic bottles with rubbish and make eco-bricks. We then build eco-structures out of our eco-bricks. At that moment, a spark came into his eye.

I had to leave the next day so I was not able to give him any more information. The following year, when I returned, he had built a little environmental centre. I saw that he was motivated so we had a discussion about building something more. After some debate, together we came up with the idea of creating an eco-restaurant. He had some spare space on his land and so we agreed that we could build it there.

Why did you choose to build an eco-restaurant?
When I talk to schools and community groups, I often talk about the dolphins and their plight. We might throw away a piece of rubbish and then the wind can pick it up and dump it into the river. The river takes it down to the ocean. Along comes a dolphin and, thinking it is a jellyfish, mistakenly eats it until their stomachs are so full of plastic that they die. I ask how many people love dolphins? Everyone loves dolphins and so that's shocking for them. Also there are lots of birds, turtles and other animals that are dying because of our rubbish.

The solution? Let's stop the rubbish getting to the ocean in the first place and build something with it instead! So, we make eco-bricks; plastic bottles filled with all kinds of landfill rubbish; like plastic bags, polystyrene, broken pens etc. So, firstly, the eco-restaurant is about using up rubbish as it is built with these eco-bricks.

Secondly, restaurants normally use polystyrene cups and plates which produce a huge amount of rubbish in the area. We use natural banana leaves instead to serve the food. We sell fish wrapped in banana leaves, and empanadas – which is cheese wrapped in a kind of fried dough and little rice balls. Also, everything else is washable or consumed in the restaurant.

And thirdly we do not sell anything in the restaurant that comes from a corporation such as Nestlé or Coca-Cola. The money these corporations make does not help Ecuador and is one of the reasons the local people remain poor. Without supporting local farmers and business all the money goes overseas. In addition, the local Coca-Cola company burns a huge amount of plastic so they are contributing to the contamination of the air that people breathe. And the rate of diabetes has gone up because of the high sugar consumption; sometimes you even see mothers giving tiny babies Coca-Cola.

It's totally crazy that there is so much coffee grown in Ecuador and there is nowhere you can get a cup of local coffee; Nestlé exports the coffee beans which are roasted abroad and that is where all of the money is made. Hardly anyone seems to have put their mind to roasting the coffee beans locally. We found a small-scale group called Aroma Amazonica who were just starting up. They roast beans in preparation for the coffee. We are their first customer. It's a similar story for cacao beans which are dried for chocolate. Our new drink – now locally famous and called "Moka" – is actually the true taste of the Amazon.

When I spoke with the local mayor about our idea of an eco-restaurant he said, "Wow, that's a great idea!" I asked him how many little cafés and restaurants there are in the province and he said there are thousands. When I asked him where I could buy a cup of local coffee he said, "Nowhere!! What a good idea!"

How did you build and run the eco-restaurant?
The eco-restaurant is very much a community project. Don Walter helped to arrange volunteers from local colleges, schools and the police; we often had over 50 people helping and on one day we had 75 students working on the project. These are known as large 'mingas' which are community work days. I organised all of this through Don Walter. The project was supported by the local council who provided the roof, sand, cement and 1,800 bricks for the patio. Petroecuador (the national oil company), which has the only plant nursery in the area, donated 200 plants for a garden. The local radio stations advertised the opening for free and the region's mayor was greatly supportive of the project.

The eco-restaurant and surrounding garden walls now contain 3,200 plastic bottles filled with rubbish. This is the first bottle restaurant in Ecuadorian Amazon.

There are 10 local women, all mothers, who have been involved in creating and running the restaurant, they have all helped in different ways. For instance, one mother concentrates on making lemonade. She goes to a lemon tree, picks all of the lemons and creates lemonade from lemon, sugar and water.

The eco-restaurant is very much in the early stages. The

weekends are when it's really busy because everyone comes with their kids to the river and there is no other restaurant around. So the idea is that we will open at weekends and build up during the week days as custom builds.

Volunteers working on the garden area.

What challenges did you face?
The main challenge I have is never having enough time. It takes an awful long time to get things done in Ecuador. Every day I am working with the local council and there are so many official documents – the bureaucracy is a nightmare to work with and often I feel that I am going around in circles. The phrase "mañana, mañana" is often used by locals ("tomorrow, tomorrow"), and this is famous throughout South and Central America.

In our team we have an engineer who is a local guy and he is very supportive of the project. He works for the local council and is quite high up so he is able to pull quite a lot of strings for us, but he still won't make any decisions without me. That's so frustrating. All of the main people in our team won't do anything without my authority and although I have tried to encourage them to get on with the work when I am not there, it all grinds to a standstill unless I start cracking the whip.

The council originally put an asbestos roof on the eco-restaurant and I was horrified and just said, "no, this will not do". We cannot have an ecological centre with an asbestos roof so we need to replace the roof which we are now doing.

What kind of publicity has come from the eco-restaurant?
Not only is the eco-restaurant valuable in itself, it also acts as an Information Centre where there are photos and information about rubbish, where it goes and what it does. And how to build with eco-bricks. There is also an explanation about why we do not see products from Nestlé and Coca-Cola. And so the challenges are all worth it.

I have been interviewed by numerous radio stations and TV channels about the eco-restaurant. And I have spoken to schools, colleges and other groups about the work. It has been a great opportunity to speak publicly about the issue of rubbish, supporting local food and farmers and boycotting Nestlé and Coca-Cola so that people are informed. Before I started, nobody knew there was anything bad about Nestlé or Coca-Cola – it's never been a question to local people. But as people started to take an interest in what I was doing, mayors from other regions have come to ask if I would do the same in their towns.

* * *

Nicola Peel is a committed environmentalist, working in the Amazonian region of Ecuador, helping to bring sustainable development and promoting life-styles in harmony with the Earth. Websites: www.nicolapeel.com / www.eyesofgaia.com

PART FOUR

NATURE'S POWERS & WONDERS

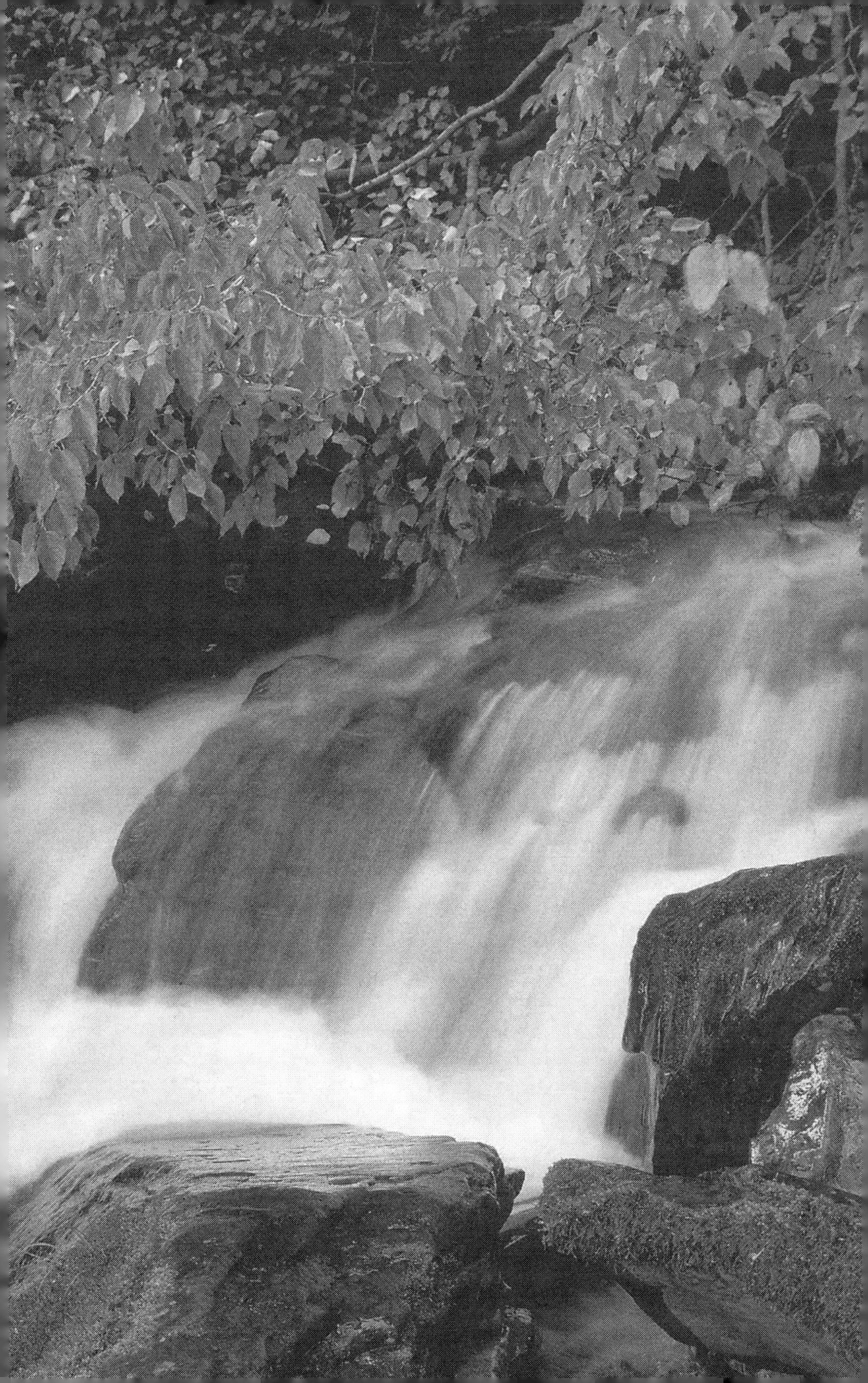

14
Living in the Paradox of Destruction & Creation

Chris Clarke

At the heart of Creation Spirituality lies the encounter with both light and dark in Nature. I want to examine this through my experience in GreenSpirit, through our current scientific knowledge, and through the work of writers such as Annie Dillard (to whom I will turn later).

Some time ago, I was explaining GreenSpirit in a casual conversation, and I suggested that many of our members looked to the natural world for the source of their spirituality. My acquaintance thought about this for a while and then asked, "How can you do that, when the natural world is filled with so much destruction, pain and violence?" I forget what I said, but I know it failed to convince! His question points to a paradox at the heart of GreenSpirit, which I want to address here by seeing it as one aspect of a much wider paradox of being human.

Being human is torn with contradiction – to which writers

over the ages have attested:

> *For the good that I will to do, I do not do; but the evil I will not to do, that I practice.*
> – St Paul

> *Oh chosen love, Oh frozen love, Oh tangled of matter and ghost.*
> – Leonard Cohen

> *There is a crack in everything; that's where the light gets in.*
> – Leonard Cohen

> *I have discovered that the place where you [God] are found unveiled is girded about with the coincidence of contradictories.*
> – Nicholas of Cusa

... and many more.

As Isabel Clarke wrote in a previous GreenSpirit magazine,[1] this universality of contradiction and paradox is a natural consequence of the New Human Story now told by cognitive science, about how our mind is constructed. She described how,

> *there are not one but two meaning making systems at the apex [of the human mind]. The verbally coded propositional subsystem gives us the analytically sophisticated individual that our culture has perhaps mistaken for the whole. However, the wealth of sensory information from the outside world, integrated with the body and its arousal system is gathered*

together by the relational subsystem, which looks after our relatedness, both with others and with ourselves.

Whenever we engage with the world deeply, with our whole person, then this 'crack' in ourselves is reflected in a paradoxicality, a 'coincidence of contradictories', in the way the world presents itself to us. If paradox is not there, it is usually a sign that we are engaging too shallowly: either thinking purely intellectually, or just basking unreflectively in surface appearances (though it might just be a sign that we have transcended this polarity – the idea behind the Zen use of paradox). So when I am inspired (given spirituality) by the natural world, paradox is often part of this.

I can draw an example from our local GreenSpirit group, which in most years spends a night in the New Forest sleeping out under the stars. At one event, as often before, I led everyone in singing and dancing to the words "Be still and know both day and night, be still and know that dark and light, are one holy circle". At this moment I know intuitively that the interplay of creation and destruction, with the pain that this often involves, is the very fabric of the Universe and is holy and right. There is a truth here, although it might stand at odds with many 'facts' about the way the world is. In reflecting on this, the cognitive subsystems model gives me a well-founded reason to trust my gut intuition, because intuition comes from the relational system, and this system is directly in touch with my senses and my body-felt relationships, with the web of connections of which I am a part. This system has evolved to give me reliable information about my place in the world, and so I have the confidence to take seriously what it tells me, even though it is paradoxical. Underlying all this is the idea that life, when it is truly flowing in us, is a dance between the two systems working seamlessly together, in which the propositional gives us our precious individuality and our ability to operate effectively in the world, and the relational gives us our oneness with the world that makes life meaningful.

When we are faced with a paradox, there is no need to give up. Often the paradox carries a strong emotional charge to alert us to its inner message. Rather than shying away from it, we can be inspired by it, and so learn to step back with our logical propositional system. We can then start to 'listen' attentively to what the web of connections is telling us through our relational system. This interplay is at the heart of Matthew Fox's Four Ways of Creation Spirituality, with the stepping back of the propositional linking with his *Via Negativa*, and the subsequent communicating message and voice of inspiration working through the relational linking with his *Via Creativa*. Much of the practice of GreenSpirit groups encourages this process through creating appropriate rituals. In this way the paradox is not evaded but embraced and transformed into an opportunity for bringing the parts of our mind together into effective action.

Let me now return to apply this to the question posed in the conversation with which I started. My acquaintance was a humanist, with a well-developed moral sensibility, caring for his fellow humans as well as for the environment and more-than-human life. Morality was an essential part of his spirituality. When he looked at the natural world, however, he saw both beauty and destruction, both good and evil: the picture was morally ambiguous. Morality had to come from elsewhere. For him it came from the highest aspirations of humanity, while for others it might come from religious teachings. From here a vast literature on morality and ethics tries to establish a basis for morality within the logical terrain of the propositional system,[2] but at the cost of ignoring the wisdom of our relational system. The outcome of such considerations is usually an eternal moral code that cannot deal with the constantly evolving world that the new Universe Story gives us. We are seeing in the globalised society of our world a hostile gulf growing between the religious fundamentalists who cling to fixed moral codes with an increasingly fearful desperation, and the consumer society that is left with no moral roots and drifts into increasing anarchy. We need a new ground for morality, as part of our spirituality.

By recognising our connections with the Earth, operating through the relational system, through a different way of knowing, morality is placed on a quite different foundation. As I acknowledge the web of connection, and open myself to what it is saying, my boundaries become porous to the world around me. I begin to connect at a bodily, material level with the world. I know myself as both an individual with the capacity for creative action, and also an integral part of a greater whole. When I encounter another person, or any other being, the rigid distinction between 'me' and the human or other-than-human in front of me dissolves: I can now do no other than act compassionately towards what is now a being of my own flesh. Even more, the challenge of this encounter with a being who is both intimately connected with me and still other than me, challenges me with "responsibility for the Other, a condition of being-for".[3] This is the root of morality.

At this point, however, a second question arises, the question on which Annie Dillard meditates throughout her *Pilgrim at Tinker Creek* – not an intellectual question, but a question flowing from the relational. She does indeed open herself to connect with the world around her. She does indeed feel compassion for her fellow creatures – and it is this that makes life so intolerable:

> *Evolution loves death more than it loves you or me... We value the individual supremely and nature not a whit. It looks for the moment as though I might have to reject this creek life unless I want to be utterly brutalized. Is human culture with its values my only real home after all?*[4]

There can be no intellectual answer to this much deeper question. One can only point to those who have wrestled with its pain, who have allowed themselves to be emptied by it, and who have discovered that life itself is more powerful than the destruction that it contains. But there is no certainty here. For there are those who have been overcome by suffering and left in despair. But perhaps a clue comes from another part of our web of connections, our connections with human society. As well as individuals, as well as a part of Gaia, we are a part of many human societies and sub-societies, and where such a society is a vibrant and living whole it can transform and hold suffering that the individual cannot. Dillard's world appeared a very solitary one, which left her alone with what was often an unequal struggle. People need people, as well as Gaia.

An Earth-based morality starts with the individual opening to the Earth. But this morality then demands that it continue through human society and influence the propositional, rational part of ourselves in order to function with a moral impulse in harmony with the relational. Ethical principles, legal codes and juridical systems are all vital, but they need an awareness of spiritual interconnections with the Earth and all the paradoxical combinations of destruction and creation of Earth's evolution and life. Ethical principles arising in this way are not restricted to the human world: other beings take their place in an inclusive community. As Thomas Berry has written:

> *There is no such thing as a 'human community' without the earth and the soil and the air and the water and all living forms. Without these, humans do not exist. There is, therefore, no separate human community. Humans are woven into this larger community. The large community is a sacred community. The earth is a very special sacred community.*[5]

References
1. GreenSpirit magazine, Spring 2004, 6:1.
2. Perhaps the best attempt on these lines, in a theistic version, is in George Ellis and Nancy Murphy's *On the Moral Nature of the Universe*, Augsburg Fortress, 1996.

3. Bauman, Z. *Life in Fragments*, 1995, quoted in J Crawford's *Spiritually Engaged Knowledge: The Attentive Heart*, Ashgate, 2005, p.67.
4. Dillard, Annie. *Pilgrim at Tinker Creek*, Harper's Magazine Press, 1974, p.176.
5. Quoted in Crawford, p.204.

* * *

Chris Clarke is an author on and teacher of science and spirituality. He was a physicist at the University of Southampton researching into cosmology, quantum theory and the physics of the human brain. Since then his activities have involved leading a circle dance group, contributing to international symposia on science and religion, teaching at Schumacher College, serving on the council of GreenSpirit and running workshops for a local group. His books include *Weaving the Cosmos: Science, Religion and Ecology* (O Books, 2010), *Living in Connection* (GreenSpirit Press, 2003), and *Ways of Knowing: Science and Mysticism Today* (multi-authored, Imprint Academic, 2005).

15
The Oak Child

Nigel Lees

I think that I shall never see
A poem lovely as a tree.

This is the start to the poem *Trees* by Joyce Kilmer, which has always touched me ever since I read it as a child. Recently, I heard it on the radio sung by Paul Robeson in his rich, deep, brooding tones. Memories of childhood, which I thought I'd forgotten, came flooding back…

How old was I when I could crawl up into the belly of that old oak standing alone in the playing fields? Eight, nine, ten years old, something like that. I was small then although it was still a bit of a squeeze to make my way from her roots to the top of her trunk where I would finally emerge. I didn't rationalise it then but to me the hollow oak was always a 'her'.

I can remember the mouldy, musty, damp smell of the hollow oak, even during the long hot dry summer holidays of my selective memory. The oak with a very large root system and deep tap root survives well in dry environments. With the poetic and allegorical pretentions of an adult I would describe being inside the oak as feeling the 'embrace of her womb', but to me as a child it was a place to hide. She was a hollow oak tree and that was magical enough for me.

I knew nothing of evolution, the age of the Earth or the deep time of the Universe, but I knew that my oak tree had special powers and could transport me across the cosmos. I used to play this game of imagining myself inside a living spaceship which just happened to be made of oak. The hollow insides became a control panel and I could close up the root entrance and the trunk exit and take off into the solar system. She would transport me at great speeds and with her huge prehensile branches deflect passing meteors or comets. I could land on any planet and explore. On a number of occasions I would be chased by aliens, but my oak tree would rescue me and carry me back to Earth. One of my favourite trips was through time (Dr Who had just started then) and I would go into the past and help people escape (usually young boys like myself) from wicked barons, soldiers or evil wizards or witches. Everything was possible then.

The Mystic Oak

Like Yggdrasil, the World Ash of Norse mythology, the oak tree was also an Axis Mundi, a link between Earth and the cosmos. The oak, being one of the tallest and largest trees in the wood (it can be over 100 feet tall and more than 30 feet round), and having a low electrical resistance due to high water content, is prone to dramatic lightning strikes. It was believed by many of the peoples of Northern Europe that the thunder god, Thor, came to Earth during these storms, thus uniting heaven and Earth. The oak was sacred to him. It is not uncommon for oaks to be hollow and as such they have sometimes been visualised as a way to other realities. Southern Europe also held the oak tree to be sacred. The ancient oaks at Dodona in Greece were said to be a place of oracle and divination and dedicated to Zeus, that other wielder of lightning and storms. It is not surprising, therefore, that oaks were seen as divine doors to other worlds.

The mysterious people we call Druids, who were around before the Romans arrived in these Isles, also revered the oak tree. Though little is known about them the oak seems to have played a major part in their rituals. This is not surprising as the oak can live up to 1,000 years, is one the strongest of trees and has over 300 species. Its wood has very many uses and is known to survive fire, drought and attack by pests. One derivation of the word Druid is said to mean 'oak-knower' or 'oak seer of truth'. As a young boy playing in his hollow oak, I didn't consider myself a Druid, but in my own way I knew the tree was my doorway to adventure.

The Immortal Oak

Nature is full of wonder and surprises. Take the example of the tiny Gall Wasp. She lays her eggs on oak leaves and the biochemicals secreted by the larvae produce a reaction in the oak tree. A large swelling develops which is known colloquially as an 'oak apple'. This manufacture of the tree is a marvellous thing, though the biological pathways are complex and not entirely clear. Not only does it provide protection for the growing wasp larvae, it also helped to write history. Literally. Oak apples are incredibly high in tannins and when boiled up with iron salts and filtered they produce a very dark, permanent ink. This ink, called iron gall ink, became the standard writing medium in the West for well over 1,400 years and many hundreds of thousands of manuscripts were created using it. As iron gall ink is corrosive over time, manuscripts have to be conserved. A good example is the Codex Alexandrinus held at the British Library, where I worked for a number of years. This is reputed to be the oldest complete Bible and dates from the 5th century CE, very early in the Christian era. Many of Darwin's letters from the round world voyage of the Beagle were also written in iron gall ink, which is a particularly nice evolutionary link.

Little did that small boy know, travelling through time and space in his oak tree, that a tiny wasp on a huge oak produced one of the main ways for us to record our history.

The Biodiverse Oak

The true magic of an oak is not in its history or mythology but in what it really represents to the Earth today. Trees are the largest living organisms on the planet and collectively help us all to breathe, provide a home for millions of diverse species, hold water and help prevent erosion, provide us with sustainable timber and firewood (if cropped correctly) and produce much food and medicines for us all.

The oak tree is one of our most important woodland trees. They support hundreds of species of insects, birds, rodents, mammals, fungi, mosses and a bewildering array of microorganisms. The oak is reputed to support more species than any other woodland tree: at one published count she supports 284 species of insect and 324 species of lichen. She is an ark of biodiversity. Back then, hiding in her trunk, I would carefully try to avoid all the beetles, tiny worms, spiders and other nameless creepy crawlies. Sometimes I would hear noises inside and see piles of carefully excavated wood dust, perhaps of some tiny creature also setting up home.

However the real mystery of all trees, indeed most plants, lies beneath the surface of the soil. A symbiotic web of root and fungi called mycorrhiza, supports and is in turn supported by the plant. The tree provides complex carbohydrates to the mycorrhiza and receives, by way of exchange, many nutrients needed for growth. Mycorrhiza also facilitate a more efficient uptake of water than by roots alone and confers some resistance to disease. The oak has a very extensive mycorrhizal network and is one of the trees that are dependent on this fungal symbiosis for its very survival. Healthy oaks mean a healthy forest. Though mycorrhiza was first studied in the late 19th century, it is only within the last 30 years that we are beginning to see its real interconnectedness with the natural world. Much of the Universe is hidden to us and that is the same of this invisible plant kingdom. Poetically we might say that the oak tree is a 'universe in a forest of universes' because of its interconnected relationship with mycorrhiza. The ecologist James Merryweather put it more bluntly when he commented that a tree without mycorrhiza is a dead tree.

Many years and a lifetime later I was given the opportunity

to reconnect with the spirit of my oak child. Sitting next to a large oak one summer I wrote my own homage to the tree I love. She was my Axis Mundi, my centre of the cosmos.

Tree Meets Me

Robin speak to me of oak
Tell me her name.
Is it growth, the how of her
Is it love, the why of her
Is it now, the where of her.

Oak speak to me of Robin
Why does he move me so.
His song rings through your arms
And rings through me.
He is an echo from your past
He is a siren to your future
He is singing now.

Why do you shine so
With your patterned trunk,
Lifting up the moss and
Growing your world.
A community of beings rest in you
A galaxy is born because of you.

Useful Reading

Hageneder, F. *The Heritage of Trees: History, Culture and Symbolism*, Floris Books, 2001.

Tudge, C. *The Secret Life of Trees: How They Live and Why They Matter*, Penguin Books, 2005.

Merryweather, J. *Meet the Glomales: The Ecology of Mycorrhiza*, British Wildlife 13: 86–93, 2001.

*   *   *

Nigel Lees lives in Chepstow in Wales and is an Interfaith minister, gardener and poet.

16
The Hurricane

June Raymond

A force ten wind is officially described as a storm but a force fourteen is a hurricane. I know this because living on the Hebridean island, Erraid, these things mattered. We withstood the storms pretty well as the buildings had been designed to cope with them and I found them one of the more exciting features of island life. Only once did we have a hurricane and even then we had relatively little serious damage. But it was a different animal. One of our heavy wooden outdoor loos, which took four men to carry, was not properly secured and was lifted and moved several yards across the ground. It felt good to be safely inside a sturdy stone cottage!

My next encounter with a hurricane was a very different affair. I had gone with a friend to make a camping retreat on an uninhabited island a little further south, one of the Garvellachs. A local fisherman took us out on his trawler and we climbed up the steep side of the island to our camping ground. We put up our tents and cooked our supper on a camp fire. The weather was dreadful, lots of rain and wind and no sun. I had a strong and serviceable sleeping tent which kept me dry, once I had learnt which way to point it. My friend was less fortunate and her tiny bell tent was a constant problem. During the day we had a larger tent but because of the difficulty of carrying so much equipment we had only brought its outer shell. Nevertheless it was a wonderful and exciting way to make a retreat and I never remember hearing a word of complaint from my friend who was less used to Hebridean weather than I was. We explored the island and found ancient beehive cells built by monks who were, alas, routinely murdered by marauding Vikings. There were also the roofless remains of a beautifully made stone chapel where my friend eventually took the day tent to sleep in and find some limited shelter from the driving wind and rain.

One day a couple anchored their yacht beside the island and climbed up to explore the famous monks' cells. We chatted with them for a little while until in the middle of the conversation one of the visitors looked at his watch and said, "Well, we had better be going before the hurricane arrives". My friend and I looked at each other. "Did you say hurricane?" we asked in horror. They said, yes, it was due in about twenty minutes and seemed surprised that we had no radio to keep up to date with the weather news. So off they went while we prepared ourselves for the worst. Soon we saw an ominous green-black bank of cloud appearing between the islands. We made our tent as safe as possible and sat inside and tried to meditate while the hurricane roared around us. From time to time I would go out to check that all our pegs were firmly in the ground as I knew that if even one of them were loose the tent would almost certainly be lifted up and disappear before we had time to blink.

I often learn my most profound spiritual lessons from Nature and this turned out to be one such occasion. As I tried to meditate I could find no peace only the fear of being at the mercy of the terrible wind and rain as our fragile tent was buffeted by their force. Noise and chaos reigned and when I inadvertently touched the canvas, water poured in. I realised that while I could usually find my peace in Nature now it was impossible. I had to look inside to find stillness. When I did this I was able to allow the hurricane to be a hurricane. I stopped mentally fighting the weather and found I could be in the hurricane and at peace. I was able to cope in the present moment but I could not cope with the thought that our tent might be blasted away and we would have to survive the rest of our stay with no daytime shelter. Nevertheless I now knew that if and when such a time should occur as long as I stayed totally in the moment I would still have all I needed to cope. Thankfully it never came to this, and just as I arrived at that moment of peace and confidence my friend did the same and we looked at each other and laughed out loud.

Whatever it was I had gone to the island to learn was in that experience. The next day the sun shone and I remember lying back and enjoying its beautiful warmth and saying in my delight, "You know if heaven is better than this, I'm really not interested". And later that hurricane experience gave me the confidence to keep my peace of soul when over the next few months the chaos round about me was at a much more human level.

*   *   *

June Raymond is a sister of Notre Dame and has served as a council member of GreenSpirit for several years, is a member of their editorial and publishing team and a co-editor of GreenSpirit magazine. She lives and works in Liverpool doing healing with the Bach Flower Remedies and is the compiler of the book *Meditations with Thomas Berry* (GreenSpirit, 2010).

GREENSPIRIT
RESOURCES

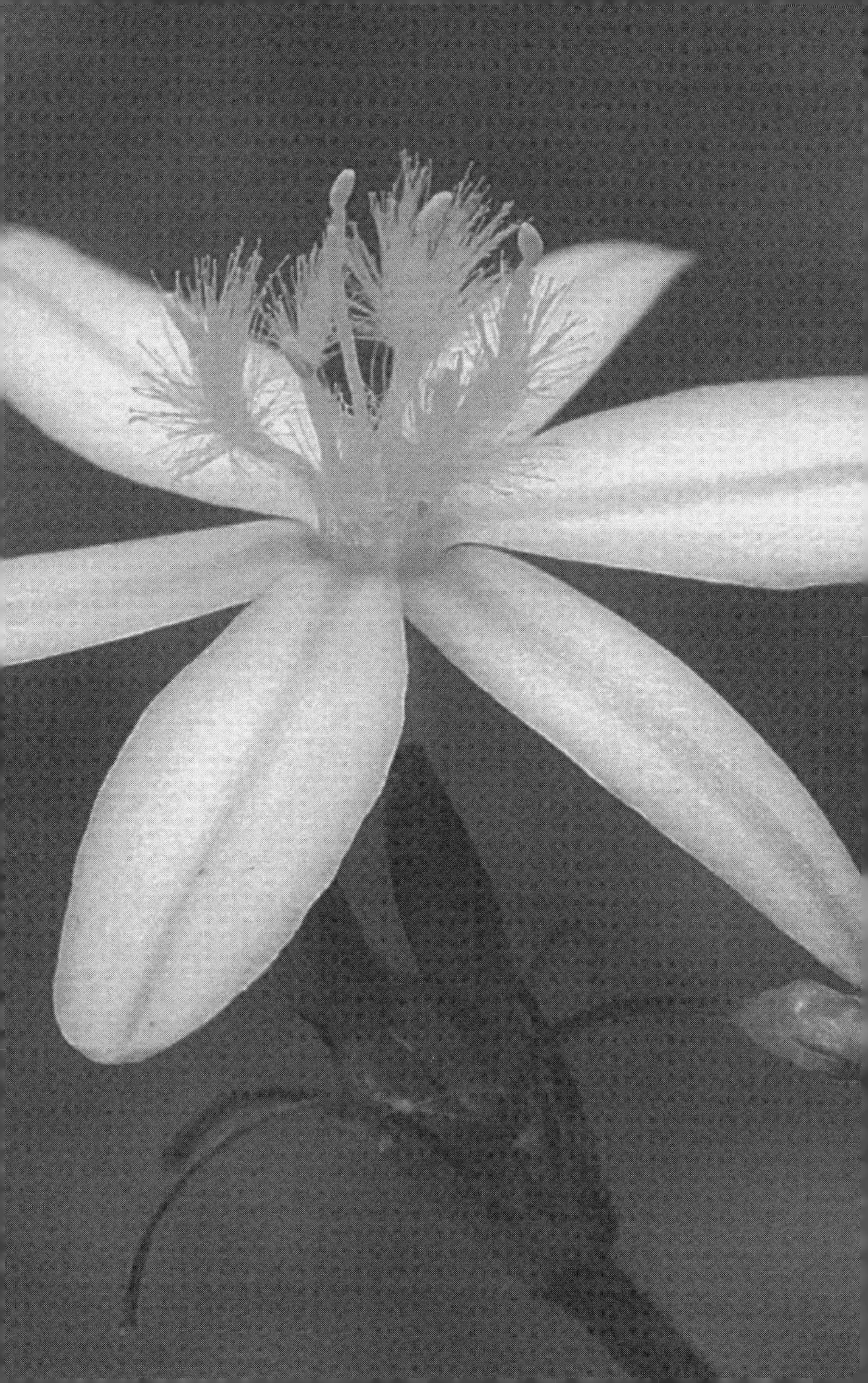

GreenSpirit Book Series & Other Resources

We hope you have enjoyed reading this book, and that it has whetted your appetite to read more in this series and discover the many and varied ways in which green spirituality can be expressed in every single aspect of our lives and culture.

You may also wish to visit our website, which has a resources section, members area, information about GreenSpirit's annual events, book reviews and much more: **www.greenspirit.org.uk**

* * *

GreenSpirit
magazine

GreenSpirit magazine is free for members and is published in both print and electronic form. Each issue includes essential topics connected with Earth-based spirituality. It honours Nature as a great teacher, celebrates the creativity and interrelatedness of all life and of the cosmos, affirms biodiversity and human differences, and honours the prophetic voice of artists.

Find out more at www.greenspirit.org.uk

"For many of us, it's the spirit running through that limitless span of green organisations and ideas that anchors all the work we do. And 'GreenSpirit' is an invaluable source of insight, information and inspiration."
~ JONATHON PORRITT

Other titles in the GreenSpirit Book Series

What is Green Spirituality? Edited by Marian Van Eyk McCain

All Our Relations: GreenSpirit Connections with the More-than-Human World. Edited by Marian Van Eyk McCain

The Universe Story in Science and Myth. By Greg Morter and Niamh Brennan

Rivers of Green Wisdom: Exploring Christian and Yogic Earth Centred Spirituality. By Santoshan (Stephen Wollaston)

Pathways of Green Wisdom: Discovering Earth Centred Teachings in Spiritual and Religious Traditions. Edited by Santoshan (Stephen Wollaston)

Deep Green Living. Edited by Marian Van Eyk McCain

The Rising Water Project: Real Stories of Flooding, Real Stories of Downshifting. Compiled by Ian Mowll

Dark Nights of the Green Soul: From Darkness to New Horizons. Edited by Ian Mowll and Santoshan (Stephen Wollaston)

GreenSpirit Reflections. Compiled by Santoshan (Stephen Wollaston)

Anthology of Poems for GreenSpirits. Compiled by Joan Angus

The Lilypad List: Seven Stpes to the Simple Life. By Marian Van Eyk McCain

Meditations with Thomas Berry: With additional material by Brian Swimme. Selected by June Raymond

Free for members ebook editions

GreenSpirit
Path to a New Consciousness
Edited by Marian Van Eyk McCain

Only by understanding the Universe as a vast, holistic system and Earth as a unit within it can we help restore balance to that unit.

Only by placing Earth and its ecosystems – about which we now understand so much – at the centre of all our thinking can we avert ecological disaster.

Only by bringing our thinking back into balance with feeling, intuition and awareness and by grounding ourselves in a sense of the sacred in all things can we achieve a new level of consciousness.

Green spirituality is the key to a new, twenty-first century consciousness. And here is the most comprehensive book ever written on green spirituality.

Published by Earth Books
ISBN 978-1-84694-290-7

'GreenSpirit: Path to a New Consciousness **offers numerous healing and inspiring insights; notably, that Earth and the universe are primary divine Revelation, a truth to be transmitted to our children as early and effectively as possible.'**
~ THOMAS BERRY (January 2009)